READY-TO-USE

Differentiation Strategies

Grades 3–5

READY-TO-USE

Differentiation Strategies

Grades 3–5

Laurie E. Westphal

 Routledge
Taylor & Francis Group

NEW YORK AND LONDON

First published in 2011 by Prufrock Press Inc.

Published in 2021 by Routledge
605 Third Avenue, New York, NY 10017
2 Park Square, Milton Park, Abingdon, Oxon OX14 4RN

Routledge is an imprint of the Taylor & Francis Group, an informa business.

ISBN: 9781032141947 (hbk)
ISBN: 9781593637057 (pbk)

DOI: 10.4324/9781003237587

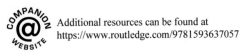 Additional resources can be found at
https://www.routledge.com/9781593637057

CONTENTS

WHAT IS
Differentiation?

"Four different lesson plans, one for modifications, one for ELL, one for on-level, and one for GT."

"Meeting the needs of all of your students."

"Altering content, process, and product."
"What does that mean?"
"You know, changing the content, process, and products that you give the students."

"This new thing we have to do now."

These are just a few of the responses I received when I recently posed the "What is differentiation?" question to various groups of teachers I spoke with while attending a state education conference. Although this question seems straightforward, perhaps it is not so simple if there is such a wide range of responses from this sampling of teachers. In fact, for many, this term has become nebulous; defining it is like putting a pin in a cloud. There are theoretical definitions, practical definitions, and even district- and school-specific definitions for the word *differentiation*. From experienced veterans to recent graduates, teachers are being given the task of differentiating instruction for their students. "My students need differentiation!" is their battle cry as they hungrily devour catalogs, visit websites, and attack booths in conference exhibit halls that address that golden word: differentiation.

Differentiation as a Teaching Lifestyle

That being said, I am not going to share another definition for differentiation; instead, I am going to focus on differentiation as a way of life in the classroom. As a theory, differentiation can be studied, analyzed, and defined, but for students to receive the most benefit, teachers have to completely jump into the role. Teaching using the differentiation lifestyle is not just differentiating this lesson or that product. A teacher who lives the differentiated lifestyle in the classroom views every aspect of his or her teaching, from the simplest to the most complex task, through a differentiated lens.

As students ourselves, we may have experienced some of these invigorating teachers throughout our school years. These are the teachers who seemed to design each and every lesson with you in mind, even though you may have been one of 150 students they instructed during the day. It seemed as if they talked directly to you and questioned you, and everyone else was just along for the ride. That is a teacher who has embraced the differentiated lifestyle in the classroom.

Not all teachers who teach this way realize they are, in fact, differentiating, because the focus of differentiation is often on the more formal, time-consuming forms of differentiation. Of course, these teachers also incorporate formally differentiated lessons (e.g., tiered lessons, menus, compacting alternatives) into their teaching; however, by embracing a differentiated lifestyle in the classroom and applying the *constructs* of differentiation in every aspect of the daily lesson cycle, from preassessments and guided practice, to independent practice and even anchor activities, the richness of the students' learning experience is compounded exponentially.

"Is This What You Want?" and the "Gotcha Factor"

It is important to note that teachers who embrace the differentiated lifestyle in their classroom may not have students who are ready for the personal freedom and independence it allows. In fact, the less students have been exposed to differentiated aspects of the lesson cycle, the more timid and insecure they may be about accepting and moving forward with differentiated tasks. Students are most familiar with the technique of ferreting out the information the teacher is seeking and then providing it, otherwise referred to as the "Is this what you want?" question. Students ask, "Is this what you want?" until they have narrowed down what the teacher is seeking, and that is exactly what they will produce and submit for grading. This behavior helps students avoid the "Gotcha Factor," which students have experienced when working on seemingly open-ended assignments. The teacher, after thinking through an open-ended assignment, has already predefined a number of correct "creative" answers. Any answer that is not one of the predetermined responses is incorrect—gotcha!

"Is This What You Want?" and the Pronoun Shift

Having experienced and often perfected the "Is this what you want?" question, many students may become confused or frustrated when a teacher who has embraced the differentiation lifestyle in his or her classroom suddenly changes pronouns. The student asks, "Is this what you want?" and the teacher deftly responds with a question that changes the pronoun, such as, "Does your work meet the guidelines for your activity?" The student is immediately confronted with a response that requires "my," "mine," or "I"—a pronoun shift from "you" (the teacher) to "me" or "I" (the student). The student may not be deterred, and it may take a few more variations on the pronoun-shifted response to the "Is this what you want?" question before the student returns to her seat knowing she will not receive the response for which she had hoped. For the teacher who is adopting the differentiated lifestyle in the classroom, the "Is this what you want?" questions can last for 1–2 months at the beginning of the school year, depending on the students' experiences and abilities. Slowly, fewer and fewer students will follow the teacher around asking the barrage of confirming questions. Instead, the teacher will begin hearing students tell each other, "You may as well not even ask, the teacher is just going to ask whether or not it follows the directions or meets the guidelines, and if we can defend it, it will be right."

Differentiation and Learning Styles

To keep things simple, I focus on four basic learning styles: kinesthetic/tactile, verbal, visual/written, and auditory. Although these learning styles are representative of all of our students, the majority of lessons and products student experience in the classroom are traditionally visual or written in nature. There are various educational reasons for this phenomenon.

First, most teachers prefer to teach and assess new information in the manner in which they themselves learn best, and most teachers are visual learners. Second, visual and written activities are usually less subjective and easier to grade. Consequently, it is easier to justify the grades students earn. Last, visual and written products tend to lead to quieter, more organized classrooms. All of these reasons are valid when it comes to offering visual or written products, but perhaps there is more to consider.

When teachers are asked to share what they perceive to be the most common learning style of their elementary students, the resounding response is usually "tactile/kinesthetic" or "verbal." Elementary students just want to touch everything! No story told by students of this age is simple—it is filled with so many "and thens" that an English professor would be mesmerized by the students' capacity to create so many elaborate run-on statements. This disconnect between lesson design and learning style has been going on for generations for the above-mentioned reasons. To be clear, tactile/kinesthetic learners can certainly work with visual strategies; however, if you really want to know how much a learner knows, you must give him an opportunity to express his knowledge through his preferred learning style.

This is best exemplified using teachers themselves as examples. Consider teachers who are attending a workshop or training and are asked to share what they know about a new concept. Which activity would tend to provide more information to the facilitator: having teachers complete a questionnaire, or asking teachers to act out a scenario for their peers? The majority of teachers would undoubtedly respond by saying a questionnaire would provide more information. Why? Responding through a written, visual format reflects the most common learning style of teachers, and therefore they are more likely to provide more complete, in-depth information. The implication of this discovery is that opportunities for students to learn new information, process what they have learned, and express their knowledge should accommodate various learning styles, including, of course, visual and written.

Selecting Activities for the Differentiated Lifestyle in the Classroom

After years of living the differentiated lifestyle as a teacher, I have had to defend the use of small, everyday, often verbal and tactile/kinesthetic experiences as a way to support differentiation theory as we know it. Many resources discuss the intricacies and implementation of differentiation and the various strategies that go along with it. This book, however, focuses on activities that support the daily routines found in standard lesson design, doing so with the words "ready to use" in mind.

As a result of the buzz about differentiating instruction, most teachers have been exposed to different concepts of differentiation. After reading a copious number of articles and books on differentiation and rethinking standard lesson designs and activities, I have brainstormed and assembled a list of criteria for activities designed for the differentiated lifestyle in the classroom. Effective differentiated activities seem to possess at least 90% of the following criteria. Differentiated activities:

- are always based on the content being studied—they serve an academic purpose;
- have a degree of built-in success for all learners;
- meet the needs of diverse ability levels without ceilings;
- are flexible and will grow and change based on students' experiences and abilities;
- encourage intellectual risk taking for students;
- generally have more than one "right" answer;
- provide different ways to obtain and share information;
- ask students to think and stretch;
- accommodate more than one learning style;
- allow for collaboration in pairs, small groups, or large groups;
- allow for a degree of choice;
- accept the students where they are and encourage them to move forward;
- foster responsibility and independence in action and thought;
- allow and expect instructional pronouns to change from "you" (teacher) to "me" (student);
- incorporate real-world applications whenever possible; and
- allow students to move into the highest levels of Bloom's taxonomy and encourage higher level thinking.

Not all differentiated activities or strategies will meet every criterion at once, but when analyzed, the activities selected for inclusion in this book meet at least 90% of the criteria listed above.

How to Use This Book

The strategies in this book are broken into two groups: no preparation and low preparation. Strategies requiring no preparation are those that can be used at a moment's notice and implemented without needing to create or photocopy materials. Strategies designated as having a low amount of preparation require only minor amounts of preparation, such as gathering or creating needed materials that can be used again in the future. These carefully selected strategies can be easily integrated into different phases of the lesson cycle, allowing the benefits of differentiation to be integrated seamlessly into teachers' already-prepared, often traditional lessons and units.

Strategy Pages

Each ready-to-use strategy page follows a similar format. An explanation of each aspect is included below, although not all strategies will include every aspect.

Title

This, of course, is the title for the strategy, although you should feel free to use whatever title will make the most sense to your students.

Learning Styles Accommodated

There are four learning styles addressed with these activities: tactile/kinesthetic (hands-on, acting out), auditory (listening), verbal (speaking), and visual/written (drawing or writing). All of the strategies selected for inclusion in this book meet more than one of these learning styles. The majority of the ready-to-use strategies incorporate the most common learning styles of our elementary learners: tactile/kinesthetic and verbal.

Best Practices

This section lists how each ready-to-use strategy might fit into the typical lesson cycle. A brief description of each follows.

Preassessment. These are activities that either take place on the first day of the lesson, when objectives have been shared with the students, but before any instruction has taken place, or are suggested as a curriculum compacting option.

Discussion. These strategies can be used to facilitate small- or large-group discussions, depending on the instructions that are given or the strategy that is implemented.

10–2. These strategies are those that fit nicely into the "2" piece of the 10–2 instructional technique. This active learning theory states that in order to increase students' retention and understanding of new information, the presentation of new information in direct instruction needs to pause approximately every 10 minutes to allow students 2 minutes of quality processing time before instruction continues. Traditionally, this occurs when the teacher pauses and asks students if there are any questions (and there usually are not). Strategies with a 10–2 designation replace this "Any questions?" practice and will enable students to take a few minutes to process the information that has just been presented.

Checking for understanding. This early phase of the lesson cycle is used to quickly check to see that students understand the basic vocabulary and any prior knowledge required before moving forward with the new information.

Guided practice. This term describes the teacher-supported practice found in most direct teaching models. Strategies with this designation allow for effective teacher monitoring of the practice process, often with the option of releasing students who are showing mastery into their independent practice portion of the lesson.

Independent practice. These strategies provide students an opportunity to use and extend their newly acquired knowledge and skills. Most of the ready-to-use strategies can be used individually or in small groups.

Review. These strategies focus on ways that students can revisit and process the lesson or unit's content in new and different ways than it was presented. The reviews often require students to interact in small and/or large groups.

Anchor activity. Anchor activities are made available to students after they have finished their assigned work. The anchor activity strategies can be placed at a center or in a folder students can access when they finish their work for the day. Most anchor activities are self-paced and can be completed without teacher monitoring.

Extension. Strategies that are appropriate for extensions have the option to extend over more than one day and encourage greater depth and research into the content being taught.

Description

This is a short, one- or two-sentence description of the activity.

Implementation

This section outlines the general implementation of each strategy in the classroom. Although strategies have different uses and ways they can be implemented, this section focuses on the most common use of the strategy and includes any tips or suggestions to make its implementation more effective.

Specific Uses or Ideas

This section explains all of the strategies as they relate to the best practices addressed earlier. When a strategy is selected to represent a best practice, this section will give either a general description of how it could facilitate differentiating that practice or a specific content-based example of its use in a classroom. Some of the best practices for a strategy will be obvious based on its implementation suggestion; however, many of these ready-to-use strategies can be effective in other areas with minor adjustments. Examples here will fall into the categories of: preassessment, discussion, 10–2, checking for understanding, guided practice, independent practice, review, anchor activity, and/or extension.

Materials

Although the majority of the strategies require few to no materials, any that are needed for the activity will be listed here.

Directions for Creating the Strategy

Some of the strategies require the teacher to create accompanying materials for student use. There are two different kinds of strategies included in this section: those with materials the students will use (and consume) during their activity, usually content-based questions for a specific subject, and those with materials that need to be created just once and can be used multiple times throughout the school year. These strategies were chosen with the planning and preparation process in mind; the creation phase should not take longer than 10 minutes. This section will provide the steps needed to create the materials used in each strategy.

Modifications

Although the strategies themselves are differentiated to meet the needs of the students' varying levels, teachers may want to modify the activity somewhat or allow for more independence on the part of the students. This section shares modifications that may be needed based on the needs of individual teachers and their students.

Sample Explanation

Some of the activities are accompanied by templates or ready-to-use examples that follow the strategy pages. This sample explanation may simply identify the templates that follow or provide instructions for implementing specific content examples.

Downloadable forms are also available on http://www.routledge.com/client/ downloads/differentiation.cfm.

STRATEGIES REQUIRING NO PREPARATION

3 - 2 - 1

Learning Styles Accommodated

- Auditory
- Tactile/Kinesthetic
- Verbal
- Visual

Best Practices

- Preassessment
- Discussion
- 10–2
- Independent Practice
- Anchor Activity

Description

- In 3–2–1, students use these numbers to determine the amount of information they need to brainstorm or record related to the concept being studied.

Implementation

- The students are asked to write the numbers 3, 2, and 1 down the left side of their paper, leaving space beside each number.
- Once they have done this, students are given specific ideas to brainstorm beside each number. For example, when using 3–2–1 as a ticket to leave class, students may be asked:

  3: Record three important terms or words you have learned today.

  2: Write two ideas you would like to explore further.

  1: Describe one skill or concept you have mastered today.

Specific Uses or Ideas

- *Preassessment*: 3–2–1 is a quick form of preassessment that can be used as a variation of a traditional KWL chart. Students could be asked:

    3: Record three things you think you already know about this topic.

    2: Write two things you need to know about this topic.

    1: Explain one way this topic might be helpful to you.

- *Discussion*: In order to facilitate discussion, groups can be asked to brainstorm a 3–2–1 about the current content. The tasks for 3–2–1 should encourage evaluative thinking, which is open to discussion and debate between groups. An example of a math discussion is:

    3: Discuss three ways that people use fractions in their daily lives.

    2: Write two things you have to consider when you complete a fraction addition word problem.

    1: Develop and solve one difficult fraction addition word problem to share with your class.

- *10–2*: At the start of the lesson, students are asked to write 3–2–1 on the top or margin of their paper. They are given these expectations during the lesson:

    3: Record three new things you have learned.

    2: Write two things you think will be on the test.

    1: Explain the most important thing discussed today.

    As the lesson progresses and students take their 2-minute processing breaks, they will fill in different aspects of their 3–2–1, with the goal of having it filled in by the time the lesson is complete.

- *Independent Practice*: 3–2–1 can be used with any content as independent practice. It simply narrows the amount of work the students might traditionally complete during this phase of the lesson. For example, a social studies independent practice 3–2–1 might include:

    3: Record three ways our local government impacts our lives.

    2: Brainstorm two things that you would not have been able to do without the U.S. Constitution. How might your life be different?

    1: Write one paragraph that explains the importance of the U.S. Congress (House of Representatives and Senate).

- *Anchor Activity*: Once students have finished their lesson, they can use the 3–2–1 activity to determine how they will investigate a concept further. One example is:

    3: Write three ideas you would like to investigate further.

    2: Brainstorm two sources you could use to investigate each idea.

    1: Choose one idea from above and create a product to show what you have learned during your research.

Materials

- None

Modifications

- If more information is needed, this can easily be adapted to the "odd take-off" variation (5–3–1) or the "even take-off" variation (6–4–2), both of which require more examples or ideas.

THE BLOB

Learning Styles Accommodated

- Auditory
- Tactile/Kinesthetic
- Verbal

Best Practices

- Preassessment
- 10–2
- Independent Practice
- Review

Description

- In The Blob, groups of students answer a content question one word at a time. Prepare for lots of laughter!

Implementation

- Students are divided into groups of two to seven (the smaller the group, the easier the task).
- A group is chosen to stand in a straight line and is given a question to answer using the following guidelines:
  - o The response to the question must be a complete sentence.
  - o Each person can only say one word. If the answer is longer than the number of group members, it will start back with the first person in the group and continue.
  - o The answer must flow through the group from left to right.
  - o When the answer is complete, the next person in line must say "period" to complete the answer.
  - o If a player gets stuck after a certain amount of waiting time, she can ask the student to her left (who just said the previous word) for help.

Specific Uses or Ideas

- *Preassessment*: The Blob is a great replacement for the traditional KWL chart. Students are put into groups of four and take turns coming to the front of the room to answer a question or prompt. Preassessment prompts might include:
  - o Name one thing you know about our state's history.
  - o How does our government affect our lives?
  - o Why is it important to study fractions?
  - o How do you make a bar graph?
  - o What do you know about the scientific method?
  - o Name one question you have about space.

- *10–2*: As a lesson progresses and the teacher pauses to allow processing time, a question or prompt is given for each group to answer using The Blob. These are answered in groups without sharing with the whole class. Another option is to have one group at a time come to front of the room to answer a question about the current content. In addition to direct content questions or prompts, sample generic prompts could include:
  - o Summarize what we just talked about in one sentence.
  - o What was the most important thing we discussed today?
  - o Give one way this information applies to your daily life.
  - o Name an example of what we are studying.

- *Independent Practice*: After discussing the information presented in the lesson, groups are asked to come to the front of the room to answer questions about the material. These questions could come from the standard worksheets or reading that students would traditionally do independently.
- *Review*: The Blob can replace the processing of any traditional review sheet. In advance of the review session, give students the review questions or topics that will be covered on the assessment. Although students are not required to write responses or look up information, they should know these are the questions that their group may be asked during The Blob review activity. Students usually review the information ahead of time so they are knowledgeable when it comes to answering the questions in front of their classmates.

Materials

- None

Modifications

- The smaller the groups are, the easier this activity is for participants. Depending on the ability level of the students, it might be best to start with pairs of students and move to larger groups as students' confidence and content knowledge increase.
- Groups can be given the question they are going to answer a few minutes in advance so they can discuss the content and prepare their answer.

Learning Styles Accommodated

- Verbal
- Visual

Best Practices

- Preassessment
- 10–2
- Independent Practice

Description

- In this activity, students brainstorm and record ideas in concentric boxes. As they progress toward the center of the concentric boxes, ideas become more detailed or specific.

Implementation

- Students are asked to turn their paper landscape and draw a box using the majority of the paper.
- Students then draw another box inside the first. Depending on the size of the paper, students can usually draw up to four boxes and still have sufficient room to write or brainstorm ideas.
- Students can work individually or in groups to brainstorm and develop ideas to record in each box.

Specific Uses or Ideas

- *Preassessment*: By grade 4, a KWL chart has often lost its effectiveness as a preassessment tool. Boxing, however, can provide similar information in a different format using three boxes. Students can record ideas or words that come to mind for an upcoming unit in the outermost box; they can focus on large ideas, concepts, and even feelings that may be related to the topic. The structure of the boxes limits the amount of space in which to write, so students tend to be more concise when brainstorming with this strategy. In the next box, students can reflect on the ideas listed in the outer box, perhaps recording two or three ideas they know the most about from the outer box with an example for each. In the innermost box, students can pose one or two questions they have on the topic that will be covered, based on the information around the outside of the box.

- *10–2*: When instruction pauses for the 2-minute reflection, students can record important bits of information just presented or discussed in the outermost box. In the next box, they can record a question they have about the content. The innermost box can be filled in at the end of the lesson with an observation about or summary of the most important information presented or a final unanswered question.
- *Independent Practice*: Venn diagrams allow students to compare and contrast concepts being studied, whereas boxing allows students to analyze information from general to the more specific. For example, in a language arts class, the name of a character would be placed in the outermost box. Character traits for that character would be recorded in the next box. Finally, students would write about how these traits impacted the plot of the story or novel in the innermost box.

Materials

- Paper
- Boxing template

Modifications

- The number of boxes can be altered depending on the content or students' skill level.

Sample Explanation

- The following pages contain a sample generic Boxing template and a Boxing template that can be used to assist students in brainstorming and beginning the writing process. Both of these templates can be used as is or modified to meet the students' needs.

Boxing Template

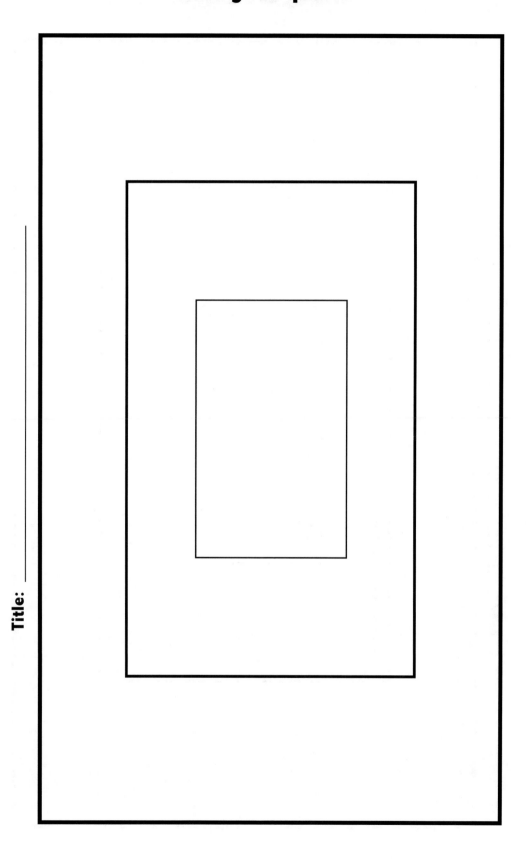

Title: _____

Writing Brainstorm

Title: _____

Here are all of the things I could write about:

Choose one. Here are details about it:

Here is my topic sentence:

CONCEPT DIAGRAM

Learning Styles Accommodated

- Auditory
- Visual

Best Practices

- Preassessment
- Discussion
- Checking for Understanding
- Independent Practice
- Review
- Anchor Activity

Description

- A Concept Diagram asks students to look at a concept from different perspectives, including examples and nonexamples, vocabulary associated with the concept, and characteristics or properties that are always, sometimes, and never present.

Implementation

- Concept Diagrams are drawn in student notebooks or reproduced and distributed for student use.
- Students can be given the same concept, or the class can be divided into groups, with each group receiving a different concept appropriate to the current unit of study.

Specific Uses or Ideas

- *Preassessment*: Students are given a concept from an upcoming unit, such as food chains. They fill in as much of the information on the Concept Diagram as they can before instruction takes place. As they progress through the lesson or unit, students can add and change information on their Concept Diagram.

- *Discussion*: Concept Diagrams work best to facilitate discussion when groups of students are given different concepts to analyze. For example, for a discussion on character traits, divide the classroom into four or five character trait groups (e.g., honest, generous, cruel, selfish). Each group should analyze its trait and identify examples of characters who have demonstrated that trait in books or stories the students have read. After the Concept Diagram is completed, each group can discuss the similarities and differences between the traits.

- *Checking for Understanding*: Concept Diagrams can allow teachers to do a quick check of student knowledge before proceeding. For example, after an introductory lesson on equivalent fractions, students would be asked to draw a Concept Diagram in their math notebook showing everything they understood about this concept before being asked to complete calculations using equivalent fractions.

- *Independent Practice*: Concept Diagrams can be used for independent practice as well. For example, after discussing the concept of communities and what it takes to classify an area as a community, students would be asked to complete a Concept Diagram on a community of their choice to show that what they have selected meets the criteria of the definition.

- *Review*: As a review, the teacher (or class) brainstorms the major concepts, vocabulary words, or themes covered during the current unit(s) of study. Each student is given a Concept Diagram and his or her own individual concept from the brainstormed list. Students then complete a Concept Diagram for their concept and share their information with their classmates through the teacher-assigned review format.

- *Anchor Activity*: When a student has finished early and wants to learn more about the topic being studied or a topic of his or her choice, Concept Diagrams are an effective way to help students stay focused on the content, while also allowing them to go further in depth.

Materials

- Paper or Concept Diagram template

Modifications

- The various sections of the Concept Diagram can be split apart. For example, students can focus on one box or one row of boxes each day, completing the entire diagram throughout the week.

Sample Explanation

- The following pages include two sample Concept Diagram templates that can be used as they are or modified to meet the students' needs. Some students prefer a format that resembles a mind map that shows connections between ideas, while others prefer a format that highlights the logical order of the Concept Diagram.

Concept Diagram

Characteristics or Attributes

Concept

Always Present

Sometimes Present

Never Present

Important Words

Examples

Nonexamples

Draw a Picture or Diagram of the Concept

Ready-to-Use Differentiation Strategies, Grades 3–5 ©Taylor & Francis.

Concept Diagram

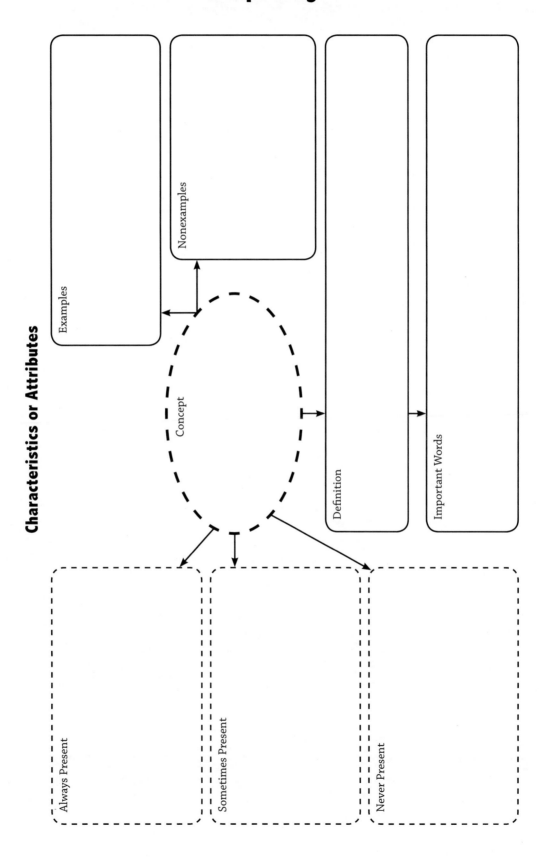

Characteristics or Attributes

Examples

Nonexamples

Concept

Definition

Important Words

Always Present

Sometimes Present

Never Present

DON'T BREAK THE BANK

Learning Styles Accommodated

- Auditory
- Tactile/Kinesthetic
- Visual

Best Practices

- 10–2
- Independent Practice
- Anchor Activity

Description

- In Don't Break the Bank, students are given a question to be answered or a short summary to be written within certain monetary limitations, in which words cost a certain amount of money.

Implementation

- The teacher will need to determine an appropriate target word range and cost for each word. If each word costs $0.10, an appropriate range might be $2.00–$2.50 (or 20–25 words). These cost ranges are explained to students.
- These restrictions reinforce careful word selection and succinct expression of ideas.
- Questions and responses can be recorded in journals, as warm-ups, or on tickets to get out of class.

Specific Uses or Ideas

- *10–2*: Shorter versions of Don't Break the Bank can be effective with the 10–2 strategy. For example, while reading a story, ask students to stop after every other page or a significant event in the story. In small groups, students will discuss what they have read and record a response to their discussion in their notebooks or journals that costs between $1.00 and $1.50, with each word costing $0.10. Names of the characters and any words found on the classroom word wall or unit vocabulary lists can be written free of charge.

- *Independent Practice*: Any independent practice in which students have to write can benefit from the Don't Break the Bank strategy. For example, after completing a science experiment on sound and its properties, students are asked to write a conclusion to their lab experience. They should spend between $2.00 and $2.50 on their written conclusion. Words from the unit's vocabulary list can be used free of charge.

- *Anchor Activity*: After finishing their assigned work, math students can be given the opportunity to write their own math problems for their classmates based on the content being studied. Students should limit their words to a budget between $2.00 and $2.50.

Materials

- Paper
- Journals

Modifications

- Using punctuation can either earn or cost money. For example, when students use periods or commas, they can add $0.05 for each use to their goal range. The more punctuation they use properly, the more words they can use to express their ideas. Conversely, if punctuation costs $0.05, the more punctuation they use, the fewer words they can use in their writing.

- Using targeted words in the writing can be free of charge or given a discounted rate. For example, when students use words from the classroom word wall or the vocabulary list for the current unit, they do not reduce the funds available for their writing. These words could also be half-price words to help encourage their use.

Learning Styles Accommodated

- Auditory
- Tactile/Kinesthetic
- Verbal
- Visual

Best Practices

- Preassessment
- Discussion
- Anchor Activity

Description

- Draw a . . . asks students to draw an intangible object or concept. They can also be asked to create a drawing to symbolize a generalization.

Implementation

- In small groups, students are given the task to draw a concept or idea. Their drawing must meet the following guidelines:
  o   Use one piece of paper.
  o   Have the option of using words.
  o   Use only three colors, and these colors must be meaningful to the drawing.
  o   Include at least five details.
  o   Be ready to share.

- Once the drawings have been created, each group should be given the opportunity to share its drawing. The group members should not only share what was drawn but also explain why the three colors were chosen and their importance to the overall concept. As drawings are shared, the teacher can ask the other class members for any questions or comments they might have, making the sharing interactive in nature.

Specific Uses or Ideas

- *Preassessment*: Before beginning a novel study, students can be broken into groups of three or four. Each group is asked to draw a different idea that might be found in the novel:
  o   Draw a hero/heroism.
  o   Draw a villain.
  o   Draw courage.
  o   Draw fear.
  o   Draw power.
  o   Draw honor.

  Once the drawings are complete (or time is up), each group should share its drawing. As different groups present, the teacher can add tidbits and information about each of the topics and how it relates to the upcoming content that will be covered in this unit.
- *Discussion*: This strategy naturally lends itself to discussion in all of its forms. Given that students are asked to draw an intangible concept (e.g., humor) or a generalization (e.g., living thing) that is open to student interpretation, discussion will naturally follow as groups share their drawings and their meanings with their classmates.
- *Anchor Activity*: For an added challenge, once students have finished their task for the day, they can work on a creating a community Draw a . . . in which each student is allowed to add one small portion to create a larger work. For example, while studying food webs and interactions, a Draw a . . . is set up in a central location. The teacher can add the first item to the drawing. Once students have completed their tasks for the day, they are allowed to add one component to an ever-growing food web that is being developed. The web will constantly change based on the plants and animals added, and students will enjoy observing the turns it takes as it develops.

Materials

- Large pieces of paper (manila or newsprint works well)

Modifications

- Students can be asked to write a paragraph explaining the significance of the different colors included in their drawings.
- Drawings can be made at the beginning of the unit and revisited once instruction has taken place to allow for changes based on knowledge acquired during the unit.

GIVE ME AN
A-B-C!

Learning Styles Accommodated
- Verbal
- Visual

Best Practices
- Preassessment
- 10–2
- Guided Practice
- Independent Practice
- Review
- Extension

Description
- In Give Me an A–B–C!, students use the letters in the alphabet to record ideas, concepts, and statements about the information being studied. Each recorded idea should begin with a different letter of the alphabet.

Implementation
- Students are asked to write the letters A through Z (or a designated portion of the alphabet) in their notebook, on a piece of paper, or on a poster.
- Students are then given a set amount of time to brainstorm words, definitions, or phrases related to the current unit of study. Each idea should begin with a different letter from the alphabet.
- Once time has been called, students should share their ideas with each other and brainstorm any letters that were left blank during the initial brainstorming process.

Specific Uses or Ideas

- *Preassessment*: In order to engage their prior knowledge during a math lesson, before any instruction has taken place, students are asked to think about fractions and brainstorm as many ideas, words, or concepts as possible that begin with each letter.

- *10–2*: Students will write the letters A through Z in the margin of their social studies notebook. As the class progresses through a unit on their state's history, students will fill in ideas, words, or concepts for each letter during their 2-minute processing period. By the end of the unit, students will have written down something for each letter.

- *Guided Practice*: In language arts, groups of students are given a large piece of paper to record the letters of the alphabet down the center of the paper. Each group is assigned a different story element or character from the book currently being read. Groups are then asked to record ideas about that element or various character traits. Once they have finished, a handful of letters can be selected at random and groups can share what was recorded.

- *Independent Practice*: Following a discussion on the importance of governmental roles in social studies class, students can research the names of important governmental officials and create an A–B–C list of these names. The list can include a brief statement about why each person's job is important.

- *Review*: Rather than using a study sheet to review for a test on physical science, students are asked to revisit their notes and create an A–B–C list of concepts covered during the unit.

- *Extension*: Any lists created during instruction could be made into individual alphabet books, or each student can contribute one of his or her letters to a class alphabet book. These books often become prized classroom possessions.

Materials

- Paper

Modifications

- Assign fewer letters to students who need modifications.
- Rather than require that each letter on the A–B–C list correspond to the first letter of the phrase or word, allow students to use it as any one of the letters found in the phrase or word.

Sample Explanation

- The following page provides a basic template that can be used with Give Me an A–B–C!

The A–B–Cs of _____

A	
B	
C	
D	
E	
F	
G	
H	
I	
J	
K	
L	
M	

The A–B–Cs of_____

N	
O	
P	
Q	
R	
S	
T	
U	
V	
W	
X	
Y	
Z	

INITIAL SENTENCES

Learning Styles Accommodated

- Verbal
- Visual

Best Practices

- 10–2
- Independent Practice
- Anchor Activity

Description

- In Initial Sentences, students are asked to create a sentence in which each word starts with randomly selected letters.

Implementation

- The teacher selects 6–10 letters at random. For added drama, the letters can be selected from a bag in front of the class as the first part of the activity.
- The letters are written in a random order in a visible location and students record them onto their own paper.
- Once the letters are chosen, students are given a question to answer or a topic on which to brainstorm. Their responses need to use each of the random letters, in the order they were written, as the initial letter of each word in the sentence.
- Students should write a complete sentence that meets the criteria of the task.

Specific Uses or Ideas

- *10–2*: At the beginning of a lesson on the events that led up the Civil War, the teacher would write eight random letters (e.g., RHFULNSD) where the students can see them. After about 10 minutes, the teacher would pause the lesson to ask each group to develop a sentence to summarize what has been discussed so far. All of the words in the sentence must begin with the random letters in their stated order. After 2–3 minutes, groups are asked to volunteer successful sentences. One example of a successful sentence is: Rebels Hated Free Union—Left Nation, Supported Davis.

- *Independent Practice*: After instruction has been given, the teacher randomly chooses 10 letters from a set of sticky notes with letters written on each one. Students are asked to write an Initial Sentence about the content being studied using the letters that were drawn. Students can be asked to use at least one vocabulary word in their sentence.

- *Anchor Activity*: After finishing a lesson, students can choose a vocabulary word related to the current lesson or unit. They will create an Initial Sentence using the letters from that word.

Materials

- None

Modifications

- Instead of giving students letters in random order, provide them with a word (like an acrostic). The goal is still to create a complete sentence.
- If students are struggling with the restrictive guidelines, the following modifications can be offered:
    o   In addition to using the given letters in their assigned order, students can include any words that are three letters or fewer in between those letters to help construct the sentence.
    o   Students can use the drawn letters as the initial letters of all of the words in their sentence, but allow them to use the letters in any order.
    o   Students will brainstorm a sentence in which the letters are used in the order given, but rather than being the initial letter of each word, the letter can be found anywhere in the word.

INTERROGATION

Learning Styles Accommodated

- Auditory
- Tactile/Kinesthetic
- Verbal

Best Practices

- 10–2
- Independent Practice
- Review

Description

- Interrogation asks students to work individually or in groups to "interrogate" the teacher about the content being studied.

Implementation

- The teacher tells students they will have a quiz or another type of individual assessment at the end of the class period to test the content being taught that day. Through Interrogation, students will be allowed to ask the teacher any questions that might assist them on the assessment.
- The guidelines for questions and responses are as follows:
  o The teacher will not tell the students what the questions on the assessment will be; however, he or she will answer all questions that are asked.
  o The teacher will only provide information that is requested in each question. If the question can be answered with a yes or no, that is the response that will be given. (This will encourage students to become effective questioners.)
  o Each group of students is allowed no more than two questions.
  o Groups are given 3–4 minutes to discuss what questions they would like to ask based on their knowledge of the content being assessed. It is recommended that each group develop at least one extra question in case another group asks the same question before its turn.

o   After the students have brainstormed, the groups take turns inter-rogating the teacher about the content that will be covered on the assessment.

o   Once every group has had an opportunity to interrogate the teacher, students receive their assessment (e.g., quiz, ticket out of class, essay question) for completion.

Specific Uses or Ideas

● *10–2*: At the beginning of any lesson, students are told there will be a quiz on the information presented during the lesson. As the lesson pro-gresses, instruction stops about every 10 minutes for groups to take a couple of moments to brainstorm a question they may want to use to interrogate the teacher right before the quiz. Certain questions may be answered naturally as instruction continues; however, any questions that still remain from the 2-minute brainstorming sessions can be asked at the end of the lesson, right before the quiz.

● *Independent Practice*: Once new information has been presented to stu-dents, introduce the "stump the teacher" version of Interrogation. In this variation, groups of students are given 5 minutes to develop content-related questions about the information that was just presented. Groups are given the opportunity to take turns trying to stump the teacher. As questions are presented, each time that the teacher is stumped, the ques-tion is referred back to the group for research during independent work time, and that group receives a point. The group that earns the most points gets bragging right for stumping the teacher for this lesson (and also has the most research to do during work time!). After each group has had a chance to stump the teacher with its questions and points have been earned, groups research the answers to their questions and then share their results with the rest of the class.

● *Review*: Before a benchmark or cumulative assessment, Interrogation can be used to help students review the concepts that may be assessed. If there are more than three objectives being covered, they can be split among the groups so the teacher is being interrogated about each objec-tive from at least two different groups.

Materials

● None

Modifications

- Groups of students can have 5–10 minutes to prepare and then volunteer to be the ones interrogated instead of the teacher.

Sample Explanation

- The following page has a sample Stump the Teacher Interrogation template that can be used as is or modified to meet the students' needs. Although not necessary for Stump the Teacher, the template can be helpful in assisting students as they develop their questions and record their researched answers.

Stump the Teacher Interrogation

Write what you already know about your interrogation topic.

_____

_____

_____

_____

_____

Write at least two questions your group will use to try to stump the teacher.

1. _____

   _____

2. _____

   _____

3. _____

   _____

   Circle the number of any question that stumped the teacher.

What resources will your group use to find the answers to your stumpers?

_____

_____

_____

_____

_____

_____

Compose the response(s) to your group's question(s) that stumped the teacher.

_____

_____

_____

_____

_____

_____

LET'S TRADE!

Learning Styles Accommodated

- Auditory
- Tactile/Kinesthetic
- Verbal
- Visual

Best Practices

- Discussion
- 10–2
- Review
- Independent Practice
- Anchor Activity

Description

- In Let's Trade!, students develop and trade content-related questions with their classmates.

Implementation

- Students are broken into groups of three or four. Each group is assigned a number.
- Each person in the group develops a question about the topic or content being studied. It could be a question for which he already knows the answer, or a question about something he is still pondering. Each person in the group must have a different question.
- Each group member writes his question on an index card and folds the card in half, so the question is concealed. The group number should be written on the outside of the card so it is visible.
- The groups are asked to stand and complete at least three different trades with classmates from other groups. Each trade should be for another card that does not contain the student's own group number. No peeking at the questions!
- After a designated amount of trades or time, the groups reassemble and open the questions they have received.

- Together, the group discusses each question. Responses can be discussed with the large group, recorded in journals, written on the cards and returned to the original group, or written on chart paper for sharing.

Specific Uses or Ideas

- *Discussion*: After discussing communities and citizenship in social studies class, students are broken into groups of four. Each group is given a different role in the community as well as different types of citizens. Students are asked to write two different statements and two questions about their role in the community or the types of citizens. Cards are marked with the group's number and traded in such a way that each group should have questions or statements from four different groups. Each group briefly discusses the questions it has received and selects one that it would like to share for discussion with the entire class.

- *10–2*: As a lesson progresses, instruction is paused after approximately 10 minutes for groups of students to brainstorm summarization questions about the content that was just covered. These questions are written on index cards as they are brainstormed. By the end of the lesson, there should be enough cards so that each member of a group has one. At this point, groups can begin trading, and discussion about the questions takes place.

- *Review*: Each group is assigned a section of the unit being covered. Students are given the task of going through that section and creating two content review questions per person. The person who writes the question should also provide the answer directly below the question. The question cards are numbered and exchanged in such a way that each group receives at least one question from every other group. The questions are placed face down in the center of the table and each group member takes turns pulling a question and reading it to the group for discussion and review.

- *Independent Practice*: Students use a set of question or task cards (see sample that follows), in which each group starts with three cards. The group chooses one card that it will keep and goes through the trading process with its other two cards, hoping to "trade up" to better options. These cards are not numbered, so once a few trades have occurred, it is possible that a group could end up with a card it wished to trade away. At the end of trading time, students will return to their group to discuss and respond to the questions they received or complete the task as stated.

- *Anchor Activity*: A center or central location, such as a box on a table, can be set up for student-generated Let's Trade! stumpers. Students can place questions that come up during the unit or extension questions into the Let's Trade! receptacle. For every question students place in the center, they need to remove another student's question and find the answer. As the answers are researched, discovered, or solved, they are posted for everyone to read. This is a great alternative to the "Great question! Let's look that up!" response to the deep, probing questions asked by students. They can put their question in the Let's Trade! receptacle to stump someone and investigate a previously submitted stumper to share with their classmates.

Materials

- Index cards

Modifications

- Rather than working in groups, individuals can brainstorm and trade cards.
- Trades can be completed randomly between different classes for added variety.

Sample Explanation

- The following page has a sample set of Let's Trade! cards that can be used as they are or modified to meet the students' needs. Groups of students will keep one card and trade the others, but after trading is finished, they must answer the question or complete the task they have received about the content or topic being studied.

Let's Trade! Cards

Write a paragraph
explaining this topic.

Create two test questions
about this topic.

Why is studying this
information important?
Write your response.

Draw a picture to show
what you learned.

Create a Venn diagram
to compare and contrast
two things discussed.

List three questions you
have about this topic.

Name three examples
of this topic.

How does this topic apply
to our daily lives?

Let's Trade! Cards

Name three facts and one fib about this topic.

List as many words associated with this topic as you can.

Name one way you could teach something about this topic to others.

Share a way to remember something about this topic.

Select the most important thing you learned about this topic.

Create a mind map about this topic.

If a book were written about this topic, what would its title be? Why?

Name two areas that could be researched further about this topic.

Let's Trade! Cards

Fill in this question for the topic: What might happen if _____? Answer the question.

Fill in this question for the topic: What might happen if there were no _____? Answer the question.

Fill in this question for the topic: If you were a _____, what would you look like? Answer the question.

Fill in this question for the topic: How many ways could you _____? Answer the question.

Fill in this question for the topic: Do you think _____ is good or bad? Answer the question.

Name something that could be debated about this topic. Which side would you take? Why?

Make a windowpane of six important words or concepts about this topic. Include a picture for each.

Create your own task card.

THREE FACTS AND A FIB

Learning Styles Accommodated

- Auditory
- Tactile/Kinesthetic
- Verbal

Best Practices

- Discussion
- Independent Practice
- Review
- Anchor Activity

Description

- In Three Facts and a Fib, a popular party game has been converted into an educational strategy as students create three facts and fib about the content being studied.

Implementation

- The teacher breaks students into groups, typically of no more than three.
- Students are asked to think about the topic currently being studied. Each group is given an aspect of that topic and is asked to brainstorm three facts and a believable fib about the given aspect.
- Once each group has finished its statements, the students will share them with the class to see if their peers can spot the fib.
- In order to facilitate the sharing, the following techniques can be used:
  - o Before each group presents, ask students to go through and number their statements, rearranging them to make sure the fib isn't always the last one read. Most groups will brainstorm the fib last, so it naturally falls in that fourth position if they read them in the order written.

o   The group should determine its reader and have that person read the numbered statements slowly, not repeating the statements (classmates will hear them again in a moment).

o   As each statement is read, students should do a finger vote (1, 2, 3, or 4) in their lap to indicate which statement they feel is the fib. Sometimes students might feel there is more than one fib, so they can have two votes (using two hands).

o   Once the statements have been read once and secret votes are cast, the reader should read the numbered statements one more time so students can confirm their votes.

o   After the second reading, students should raise their finger votes in the air. Although there often will be a majority, there will sometimes be dissenters.

o   Before allowing the group to share which statement it intended to be a fib, ask various students why they feel the statement they voted for was the fib. This question/discussion session can last as long as the teacher feels is necessary before asking the original group which one was its fib.

● Three Facts and a Fib can be shared during one class period or spread out over a unit as instruction proceeds.

Specific Uses or Ideas

● *Discussion*: After discussing a story in language arts, students are divided into groups and each group is given a different character in the book. If there are not enough characters, groups can be given important inanimate objects from the story. For example, a group could be given the animal in a survival story or the pencil used to write a letter that is significant to the plot. Each group creates Three Facts and a Fib about the character or object it was assigned. As they are shared, the focus will be on discussing the votes and inferences made from the reading.

● *Independent Practice*: During a lesson on fractions and the different ways to represent them, students are given 5 minutes to create their own Three Facts and a Fib about fractions. Students will share their statements with the class and have a discussion as an alternative to their traditional independent practice.

● *Review*: The unit being studied can be broken into sections or objectives. Each pair or group can be assigned its own objective or section for Three Facts and a Fib. If there are more objectives than groups, each group can be assigned more than one objective. Students' Three Facts and a Fib are then used to discuss and review the concepts covered during the unit.

- *Anchor Activity*: After completing their work for the day, students can create Three Facts and a Fib for information that has been covered in a lesson or unit. These can be recorded on pieces of paper and placed on a bulletin board, used as a warm-up, or even collected during the week and given to students who would like an extra challenge to solve.

Materials

- None

Modifications

- Students can work individually on their Three Facts and a Fib rather than in groups, and these items can be used on unit assessments.

YOU DON'T SAY!

Learning Styles Accommodated

- Auditory
- Tactile/Kinesthetic

Best Practices

- Discussion
- 10–2

Description

- You Don't Say! is an instructional strategy in which the teacher proposes one or two open-ended questions and students take turns sharing answers to questions in an organized manner.

Implementation

- In small groups, students stand and pass the "power object" (see below) from person to person.
- As each person receives the object, he will share a one-sentence response with the group. Samples questions or sentences might include:
  - o A focus question from the lesson, such as, "Of the three _____s we talked about, which do you feel was most important and why?"
  - o Share what you think was the most interesting fact given during class today.
  - o What did you learn during the discussion today?
  - o What surprised you about the topic we discussed today?

- After everyone in that group has shared, the group sits back down and another group will go to the front of the room for its turn.

Specific Uses or Ideas

- *Discussion*: Prior to beginning a discussion, groups are given a list of three or four questions (one per member of the group). You Don't Say! can be used to have students share their initial thoughts on the questions before they are discussed with the large group.

- *10–2:* As information is presented during a lesson, instruction pauses approximately every 10 minutes. During those 2-minute pauses, students will discuss and answer an open-ended question about what was just discussed. For example, during a lesson on a state's history, groups would consider this question: "Of all the people we have discussed so far, which one do you think is most important and why?" After approximately 2 minutes, one group can be asked to share a comment that was heard within its group that the students found interesting, and the lesson continues.

Materials

- Power objects created in advance

Directions for Creating You Don't Say!

- Choose the power object that you would like your students to use. This object can be anything your students would recognize, something giving the student holding it the power to speak.
- Some teachers like to use reproductions of school mascots or content-specific pictures (e.g., science could have pictures of flasks or graduated cylinders).
- Using cardstock or heavy paper, reproduce enough power objects for each group to have an object.
- Laminate the power objects.

Modifications

- The objects can easily be made bilingual with two sides, one in English and the other in Spanish.

Sample Explanation

- The following pages have sample power objects for You Don't Say! that can be used as they are or modified to meet the students' needs.

A "dollar" for your thoughts!

I'm the star!

You Don't Say! Power Objects

Ready-to-Use Differentiation Strategies, Grades 3–5 © Taylor & Francis.

STRATEGIES REQUIRING LOW PREPARATION

BLACK OUT BINGO

Learning Styles Accommodated

- Auditory
- Tactile/Kinesthetic
- Verbal
- Visual

Best Practices

- Preassessment
- 10–2
- Independent Practice
- Review

Description

- Black Out Bingo asks students to create their own Bingo cards using the content being studied. Once they have done this, their goal is to black out the entire card through discussion or one-on-one interactions.

Implementation

- Each student receives or creates a Black Out Bingo board. The number of squares (4–16) is determined by the amount of time available for the activity.
- Once students have created their board (as needed), they need to record vocabulary, key words, examples, and essential questions from the current unit of study onto their Black Out Bingo board. Depending on the students' levels, it works best to have the class brainstorm these ideas together and have students place their selections from the list randomly on their boards.
- After they have finished their boards, students are given a set amount of time to play Bingo in which they mingle with their classmates, answering questions and obtaining signatures. An example interaction might look like the one below:

o Anna and Jessica pair up. Anna chooses an available (unsigned) concept, vocabulary word, or key question box on her Black Out Bingo board.

o Anna reads what is in the box and then shares an example of the concept, the definition for the vocabulary word, or the answer to the key question with Jessica.

o If Jessica feels the answer is the correct, she will sign the bottom of the box that Anna just completed.

o Now it is Jessica's turn to choose a box from her own paper. If she has the same box that Anna selected, she is not allowed to choose that one. Instead, she must pick another box, read it to Anna, share her answer, and have Anna sign her paper if she believes the answer is correct.

- The exchanges continue until one student (or a designated number of students) receives a black out or time is up.

Specific Uses or Ideas

- *Preassessment*: A sample preassessment Black Out Bingo board is found on page 64. This board has extra space, which allows students to record their responses once they have been shared; the board can be turned in so the teacher has preassessment information on hand. The preassessment Black Out Bingo board is used in the same method as discussed above; however, it has the added benefit of a free space. This free space gives students a "free pass" on one of the questions on their board and instead of answering it in front of a classmate, they get to ask a question to another student.

- *10–2*: Before the beginning of the lesson, a master list of concepts, words, and ideas is posted for students. After creating an appropriate-sized Black Out Bingo board (approximately a 3:4 ratio of the number of squares to the list of concepts), students randomly place the ideas from the master list. As the lesson progresses, each time students hear one of the items they chose for their Bingo board, they place a mark beside it. When instruction pauses after approximately 10 minutes, students can fill in information about each of the boxes they have marked. At this time, if anyone has obtained a black out, the student is asked to share responses to two or three concepts that the teacher requests at random. Instruction continues and eventually everyone will have a black out.

- *Independent Practice*: To encourage problem solving and collaboration, pairs of students are given Black Out Bingo boards with various real-world word problems on them and one free space. The pairs are given approximately 10 minutes to solve the problems before beginning their interactions with other pairs. Once they pair up with another group, each pair will share one of its problems, how the students solved it, and the answer; the other pair must decide if it agrees with the answer (and therefore sign the square) or disagrees (leave the square empty). Each pair then moves onto another pair with another problem. This can be done with any content-based questions as well.

- *Review*: When using Black Out Bingo for review, the more variation is in the concepts used on the Bingo board, the better. Therefore, it works best if the list of options contains more than twice the number of boxes students will be completing. The more options there are, the more review the students will be exposed to during their interactions.

Materials

- Black Out Bingo board or folded paper

Modifications

- Variations on the content Bingo cards can be created in advance by the teacher and distributed for student use.

Sample Explanation

- The following pages offer both a generic Black Out Bingo template and a sample preassessment Black Out Bingo template that can be used as they are or modified to meet the students' needs.

Black Out Bingo

Record a vocabulary word, key word, example, or essential question in each box below. Leave enough room for a signature at the bottom of each box.

Preassessment Black Out Bingo

Using the time allotted, answer as many prompts/questions and trade as many signatures as possible. Your goal is to black out your Bingo card. Each person can only sign your card once.

Name two vocabulary words that might be found on this topic.	Name one thing you would like to learn about this topic.	Name one specific place you could find additional information about this topic.
_____ **Name/Signature**	_____ **Name/Signature**	_____ **Name/Signature**
Name one thing you will need to learn about this topic.	Free Square (Ask a question of your choice.)	How could this topic apply to your everyday life?
_____ **Name/Signature**	_____ **Name/Signature**	_____ **Name/Signature**
On a scale of 1 (*little*) to 10 (*lots*), how much do you already know about this topic? Why?	Share one thing you already know about this topic.	On a scale of 1 (*easy*) to 10 (*difficult*), how difficult do you think this topic will be?
_____ **Name/Signature**	_____ **Name/Signature**	_____ **Name/Signature**

CATEGORIZATION CARDS

Learning Styles Accommodated

- Tactile/Kinesthetic
- Verbal
- Visual

Best Practices

- Preassessment
- Checking for Understanding
- Independent Practice
- Anchor Activity

Description

- Groups of students receive a small bag of categorization cards that are sorted and discussed.

Implementation

- Separate students into pairs or groups of three, and give each group a set of categorization cards.
- Each group should sort the cards using the following guidelines:
  - o All of the cards must be used.
  - o All members of the group must be able to defend a card's placement.
  - o All members of the group must agree on a card's placement.
  - o There are no "maybe" columns.

- Once the groups have had a chance to sort their cards, the teacher can read the cards randomly and have students share and discuss their group's placement of each card.

Specific Uses or Ideas

- *Preassessment*: At the start of a unit on adaptations in science class, students are given cards with pictures and descriptions of animal adaptations. Without being given certain categories, they are asked to sort the adaptations into two groups. As they examine the animals, the groups should determine their own categories. Once everyone is finished, the categories and location of cards can be shared and discussed.
- *Checking for Understanding*: Students can be given a small set (10–12) of categorization cards about the topic being discussed. They are asked to do a quick sort based on two categories the teacher assigns. The teacher can walk by each group to confirm it understands the material before proceeding with the lesson.
- *Independent Practice*: After covering a lesson on problem solving in math class, students are given 10–15 word problems on cards. They are sorted based on the techniques that would work best to solve them. Although the goal is not to solve the problems, this could certainly be the next step required after the sorting.
- *Anchor Activity*: Once students have finished a lesson, they can create their own set of categorization cards for the content being studied. When the students have finished making their cards, they can trade and sort the cards.

Materials

- Cardstock or colored paper

Directions for Creating Categorization Cards

- Create a two-column table in a word processing program.
- Select ideas or concepts from the current unit of study that could be sorted into two or more categories. Randomly enter the ideas into the table in your document. (Students will sometimes spend time matching up the pieces of paper in hopes of determining the categories.)
- Print or copy the cards onto different colors of paper or cardstock. Using different colors will make it easier to return errant cards to their appropriate card sets.
- Cut apart the card sets and put each set into a small plastic bag.

Modifications

- The number of cards in a set will vary depending on their use, the amount of content, and the amount of time the students have to complete them. A basic set usually contains about 20 cards.
- Categorization cards can be given without providing the categories so students need to sort them and determine appropriate categories.

Sample Explanation

- The following pages contain a set of character trait categorization cards. These cards can be made at the beginning of the year and used with various stories and novels. Traditionally, students are asked to indicate character traits for the characters in their readings, or perhaps teachers ask which character matches a predetermined trait. By using these generic cards, students categorize these traits and assign each of them to the characters. The choices won't always be obvious, which will lead to inferences and defenses based on the students' reading. Although these traits could be sorted and only certain traits given for each reading, by using them all, students stretch and think beyond the obvious, which often leads to in-depth discussions.

Character Trait Categorization Cards

Brave	Expert	Logical
Cheerful	Fair	Loyal
Conceited	Funny	Lucky
Considerate	Gentle	Messy
Cooperative	Happy	Mischievous
Courageous	Helpful	Neat

Character Trait Categorization Cards

Creative	Heroic	Plain
Curious	Honest	Proud
Daring	Imaginative	Respectful
Demanding	Intelligent	Responsible
Dishonest	Inventive	Sneaky
Excited	Lazy	Thoughtful

CREATIVE CONCENTRATION

Learning Styles Accommodated

- Tactile/Kinesthetic
- Verbal
- Visual

Best Practices

- 10–2
- Independent Practice
- Review
- Anchor Activity

Description

- In Creative Concentration, students use a set of concentration cards to make connections between concepts. The more creative the connections are, the faster a student can win the game.

Implementation

- In small groups or pairs, students place their Creative Concentration cards face down on their table.
- Each person takes turns flipping over two cards. Once the cards are turned over, the student must state how they are related or a pair. This might include an obvious relationship, such as that one card is the definition and the other card is a picture of the word, or the relationship between the cards may be more abstract and creative. The student has one minute to share the relationship between cards or the cards are turned back over. If a relationship is shared and accepted by the group or other player, the cards are removed and are considered a point for the student.
- Play continues until time is up or all of the cards have been removed.

Specific Uses or Ideas

- *10–2*: In small groups, students place 8 or 10 content-area cards upside down. During breaks in instruction, groups are asked to turn over two cards. Each group now has the task of making these two cards a pair by brainstorming a relationship between the cards.
- *Independent Practice*: After discussing various animal groups and their adaptations to their habitats in science class, students are given a set of Creative Concentration cards with pictures of various animals that have different adaptations, names of habitats, and names of adaptations. Students are encouraged to make matches as they flip cards over. They could be obvious matches, such as animals and their habitats, or matches between animals with similar adaptations or habitats that require similar adaptations.
- *Review*: All concepts, examples, and vocabulary words from the current unit of study are placed on Creative Concentration cards. All cards are numbered and correspond to the Obvious Answer Key (OAK). Creative Concentration sets and their OAK are given to each pair of students. Although students can play using the obvious answers, that game takes longer and students often figure out that if they can make logical content-based connections between nonobvious cards they display, they can obtain pairs of cards in a faster manner.
- *Anchor Activity*: After finishing their work, pairs of students or individuals can use Creative Concentration to practice their understanding of the content. In this case, they are not allowed to make the obvious connections to remove the pairs of cards—only creative connections will earn them a point.

Materials

- Paper or cardstock for the Creative Concentration cards

Directions for Creating Creative Concentration Cards

- Examine the current unit of study for appropriate vocabulary words, concepts, and drawings.
- Using a word processing program, create a table and enter the paired information.
- The sets of cards can be printed or copied onto different colors (when an errant card is found, it can be returned to its similar-colored mates) and cut apart.
- Each colored set can be placed into a plastic bag.

Modifications

- Cards can be numbered and answer keys provided for obvious matches.
- All cards can be designed without an obvious match to foster creative associations between the concepts being studied.

Sample Explanation

- The following page shows a sample set of Creative Concentration cards for measurement. Although there are obvious pairs of cards, students may create their own relationships between different cards as they are turned over, thereby allowing the removal of the cards that they have selected.

Measurement Creative Concentration Cards

Millimeter	Ten pieces of paper
Centimeter	Fingernail
Meter	Doorway
Kilometer	Walk in about 12 minutes
Gram	Paperclip
Kilogram	Dictionary
Milliliter	About 20 drops of water
Liter	Average size of soft drink

CUBING

Learning Styles Accommodated

- Tactile/Kinesthetic
- Verbal
- Visual

Best Practices

- Discussion
- 10–2
- Independent Practice
- Review
- Extension

Description

- Cubing is a tactile/kinesthetic strategy in which students create and/or roll a cube and answer questions to show what they have learned.

Implementation

- Divide students into groups of three or four.
- Each group receives a cube. The cube may have a question, a task to be completed, or a product to be created listed on each side.
- Students take turns rolling the cube and addressing the question or task on which it lands.

Specific Uses or Ideas

- *Discussion*: The teacher or groups can use cubes to facilitate discussions. When using them with groups, students are given a cube with content-specific discussion questions on each side. One person in the group rolls the cube, and each member of the group takes turns answering and discussing the question or statement upon which it landed. The next person in the group then rolls the cube, and discussion continues until everyone has had an opportunity to roll the cube. If the same side comes up more than once, students should answer or discuss their responses in a new and different way. When using the cube in a whole group to facilitate discussion, the teacher asks one person to roll the cube for the class. The student reads the side upon which it lands, and this becomes the topic for the whole-class discussion.

- *10–2*: Students are divided into groups of three or four and are given a cube with content questions on it. These questions could be specific open-ended questions about what is being discussed, or generic questions such as, "What is an example of something that was just presented in the lesson?" When instruction pauses for processing during the lesson, one member of the group rolls the cube. Each person in the group must then provide a different answer to the question on which it lands. If time allows in the 2 minutes, the cube can be rolled again.

- *Independent Practice*: Once students have been given instruction on a concept, they can create their own cube of information. Cubes are effective ways to show:
  - o   different content vocabulary words with drawings on each side;
  - o   story elements including author/title, setting, plot, events, or characters;
  - o   different student-developed word problems on the math concept being studied;
  - o   a who, what, where, when, why, and how prewriting activity; and
  - o   different examples of what was discussed during the lesson.

- *Review*: Cubing is an effective way to have students review concepts covered during a unit of study. Review cubes can be either teacher- or student-generated. Any questions or practice problems that would traditionally be placed on a review sheet can be easily placed on cubes. It works best when the content can be separated into skills or sections. A cube (or two, if there is a lot of information) can be created to review each skill or objective that will be covered on the assessment. These cubes can then be placed around the classroom and groups of students rotate through the cubes to review. The review rotations should have students staying with one cube no more than 10 minutes so there is a lot of movement and the students stay engaged with the activity. Students can also develop review cubes. Each group is given a section or skill that will be covered on the assessment. Using the cube template, each group develops a cube of review questions or practice for its classmates. Each cube that is developed should have an accompanying answer key. Once all of the cubes are designed, the students rotate through each other's cubes, responding to and discussing the questions presented on them.

- *Extension*: A cube can be a product or extension in itself. Students can research a topic and record their ideas on the sides of the cube. For example, a state history cube product could include:
  o Side 1: "State Stats," including population, state flower, state flag, state pledge, and other information.
  o Side 2: State motto with its meaning to the student.
  o Side 3: State government, which would include the people found in the state government and their positions.
  o Side 4: State map with major cities and landforms noted on it.
  o Side 5: State resources and their uses.
  o Side 6: State history, including a brief description of major historical events that have occurred.

Materials

- Cube template

Modifications

- Product cubes can be created using different colors, with each learning style having its own cube. Each time students roll a cube, they have to roll a different color so they will be completing products from different learning styles.
- Any questions or tasks that can be put on a cube could also be listed and numbered. Then students roll a dice and complete the activity or question that matches the number they rolled.

Sample Explanation

- The following pages have sample cubes that can be used as they are or modified to meet the students' needs.
- The first cube is a proofreading and editing cube. This cube has suggestions that can be used in conjunction with proofreading or peer editing. Once students have finished their first draft of writing, they roll the cube and check what it asks for or add what it suggests.
- The second cube is a product cube. This cube has products using different learning styles that can be placed at a center or used when different options are needed to stretch students.
- The third cube is a discussion cube. It is used during or after a lesson to allow students time to discuss and process what was introduced during the lesson.

Proofreading and Editing Cube

Reread your writing and add three adjectives to your sentences or story.

Find two sentences that could be improved and underline them. Now improve them!

Whisper read your writing out loud to yourself. Make at least one change to improve your writing.

Circle at least two overused words (e.g., like, good, bad, nice). Using a thesaurus, find replacements for these words that improve your writing.

Place squares around all of the correctly used punctuation marks. Circle any that may need to be changed.

Read your work from end to beginning, one sentence at a time. Underline two sentences that could be improved. Now improve them!

Product Cube

SKIT

Poster

Cartoon   Speech   Interview

Drawings

Discussion Cube

Give one example of what we just talked about.

Name one way you could teach something from this topic to your classmates.

How does this topic apply to our daily lives?

Ask the group a question you have about the topic we are discussing.

Share one new thing you have learned today about this topic.

What is the most important thing we have discussed? Why do you think so?

GO FISH!

Learning Styles Accommodated

- Auditory
- Tactile/Kinesthetic
- Verbal

Best Practices

- Discussion
- 10–2
- Review

Description

- In Go Fish!, students choose questions and prompts at random from a bag and share their responses with classmates.

Implementation

- Distribute the Go Fish! bags to students; each group should receive one bag.
- In each group, one person will start by choosing a card out of the bag without looking.
- The person who chooses the card should read that question or prompt to the group.
- Students can then either respond as a group or have the student who drew it answer, based on teacher discretion.
- The "fishing" of cards will continue until each student in the group has had a turn. If a student receives a question or prompt that has already been answered, she must answer it in a new and different way. This will eliminate the "had it already" constant exchange of cards.
- If there is enough time, have students from each group share something interesting they learned during the discussion.

Specific Uses or Ideas

- *Discussion*: Students can be given Go Fish! bags with various content-specific questions inside. Allow the groups to have one trip around the group (three or four questions, depending on the size of the groups). The teacher then takes a bag and randomly selects a question that can be opened up for general discussion. By allowing the groups to have an opportunity to process some of the questions before discussing with the whole class, the odds are that at least one group has already had a chance to answer the question and hold a discussion about it. This will allow the large-group discussion to flow a little better.

- *10–2*: During a lesson on the roles of leaders in government in social studies class, the teacher places generic bags of questions on the group tables at the beginning of class. The following questions have also been added to the bag using square-shaped cards (see Modifications below for explanation):
  o   What is the name of one local government official?
  o   If you could be a government leader, what position would you want? Why?
  o   Why are government leaders important?
  o   What is one quality of a good leader?
  o   Name a good leader in our school. Why did you choose this person?

  As information is given, the teacher stops every 10 minutes to allow students to process the information that was just presented and Go Fish! for one of the cards to answer.

- *Review*: When nearing the end of a unit, student- or teacher-generated content-related questions can be placed in the bags. This is also a great use for Three Facts and a Fib (see p. 51), Guess What? (see p. 89), or Myth Versus Reality (see p. 99) questions. Bags filled with different questions from different objectives are placed on tables for students to process. After 5 minutes with a bag, they move on to another table and a new bag of content.

Materials

- Cardstock for the Go Fish! cards
- Bags for cards (colored bags work best)

Directions for Creating Go Fish!

- Determine the questions to be included in your Go Fish! bags. These can be general questions that are used with every unit or unit-specific questions. Any question should be written in a way that allows multiple answers.
- If colored bags are available, make sets of Go Fish! cards in colors to match the bag colors. This will allow any wayward cards to be returned quickly to their bag of origin.
- Laminate your Go Fish! cards if they will be used on multiple occasions. The Go Fish! bags and cards can be stored in a plastic container, ready for their next use.

Modifications

- Two different types of cards can be used in the bags: the generic round thought bubbles, which remain in the bags at all times, and square content-specific questions. The reason for the two different sizes/shapes is to make it easier to switch the contents of the bags; the round shapes always stay, while the square cards are switched as content changes.
- Cards can accommodate bilingual learners by having the translation or visual clues for the questions on the back.

Sample Explanation

- The following pages are a set of all-purpose questions and prompts that can be placed and left in the Go Fish! bags on a permanent basis.

Go Fish! Cards

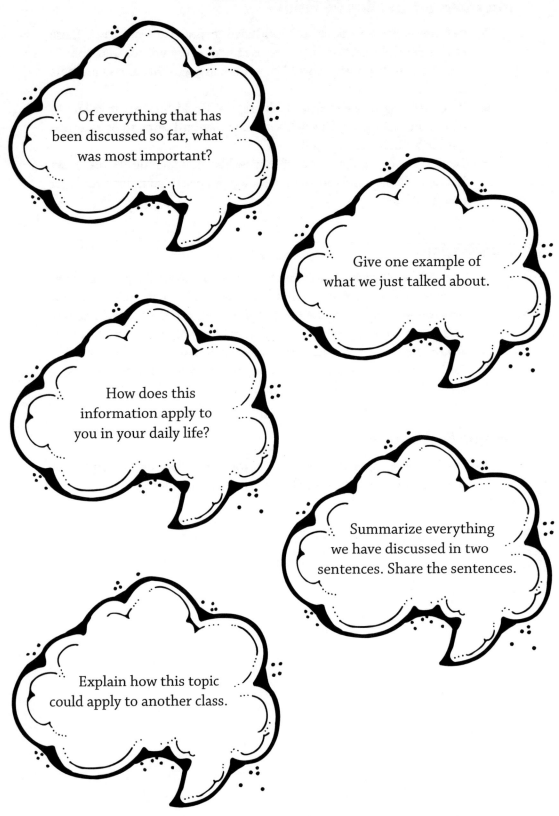

Go Fish! Cards

Thinking of the topic we just covered, what do you think we may discuss next? Why?

Ask the group a question you have about the topic we are discussing.

Give an example of a test question that would cover this material.

Share one way to help remember the information we are discussing.

Share a hand movement that could represent a vocabulary word we just discussed.

Go Fish! Cards

GUESS WHAT?

Learning Styles Accommodated

- Tactile/Kinesthetic
- Visual

Best Practices

- Independent Practice
- Review
- Anchor Activity
- Extension

Description

- Guess What? asks students to brainstorm clues that could be used to identify a target word, concept, or person. These clues are placed on a Guess What? template.

Implementation

- Assign or allow students to choose a target. Targets can include concepts, vocabulary words, or famous people associated with the content being studied.
- Students should brainstorm and record three to seven clues about their target.
- Students then rank the clues in order of how obvious they are to the identity of the target.
- After students have ranked the clues, they need to record their target word, concept, or person on the inside middle square of the template.
- From this point, clues are recorded on the inner and outer sides of the flaps surrounding the central square. It helps if students number them so it is easy to refold in order.
- The flaps are folded inward, covering the target word, concept, or person. The most difficult or obscure clue should be showing on the outside of the Guess What? template.

Specific Uses or Ideas

- *Independent Practice*: After covering life cycles in science class, students can each create a Guess What? to describe different life cycles (or the different stages in the life cycles). They can then trade these and have other students try to figure out what the target life cycle may be. After this activity, students can glue their Guess What? template into their notebooks.

- *Review*: In order to review for a test in social studies, students can each create a Guess What? with a significant person, place, or date on the inside. Rather than placing clues to the identity of the target word, concept, or person, students brainstorm test or review questions to include on the flaps. Teachers can also create various Guess Whats? for students to use to review concepts being assessed.

- *Anchor Activity*: Once students have finished with their math work for the day, students can create a target number Guess What? They choose a number as their target and record it in the center of the Guess What? template. Then they choose processes or skills covered in the current unit to include on the flaps. The problems must be carefully chosen and recorded on the flaps so users can obtain the target number as they open the flaps. They can trade or share with other students to sharpen their skills.

- *Extension*: When time gets in the way of doing a long-term research project, Guess What? can be a shorter alternative. In science, students are asked to choose a famous scientist they are interested in researching. They are told they must identify seven important dates from that person's life, why the person is famous, and how he or she impacted the world. This information can be shared through three separate Guess Whats?

Materials

- Paper
- Guess What? template

Directions for Creating Guess What?

- Students can make their own Guess What? template in a few simple steps:
    - o **Step 1:** Take the upper right-hand corner of the paper and fold it diagonally to the opposite side.

Step 1

o **Step 2:** Cut off the extra part of the paper at the bottom. When the paper is unfolded, it will be a square shape.

o **Step 3:** (a) Fold the paper into three equal sections. (b) Leaving the paper folded, now fold it into three more equal sections.

o **Step 4:** Now open the folded paper. There will be nine smaller squares.

o **Step 5:** Remove the four corners of the large square by cutting along the folded lines within those smaller squares. This will leave an interior plus sign.

o The Guess What? is now ready to be created.

Modifications

● Folded Guess Whats? can be shared with other students who try to guess the target word, concept, or person.

Sample Explanation

● The following page has a sample Guess What? template that can be used as is or modified to meet the students' needs.

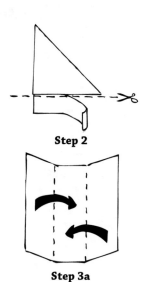

Step 2

Step 3a

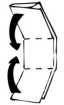

Step 3b

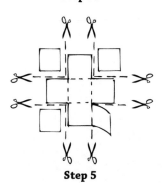

Step 5

Guess What? Template

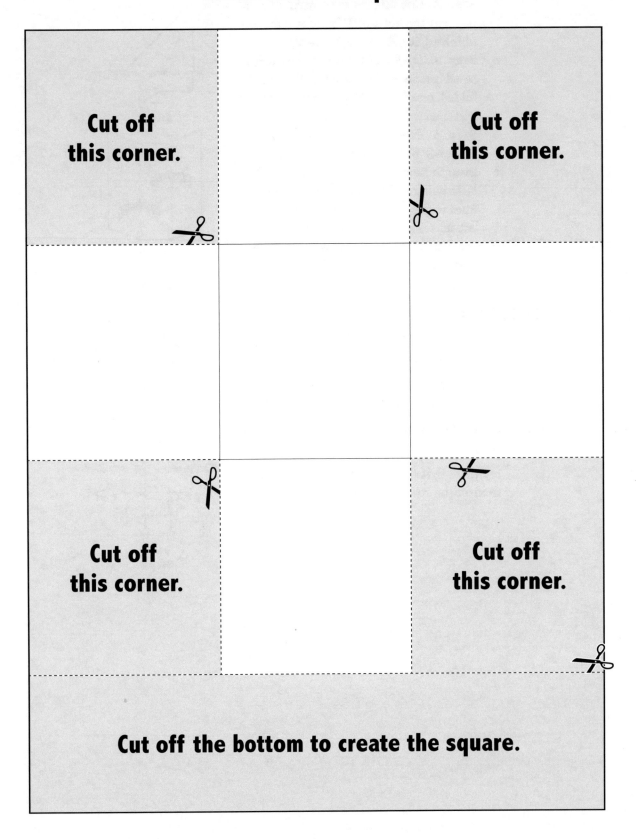

Cut off
this corner.

Cut off
this corner.

Cut off
this corner.

Cut off
this corner.

Cut off the bottom to create the square.

HANDS-ON VENN DIAGRAM

Learning Styles Accommodated

- Tactile/Kinesthetic
- Verbal
- Visual

Best Practices

- Preassessment
- Discussion
- Independent Practice
- Review
- Anchor Activity

Description

- In this hands-on variation of a traditional Venn diagram, students are given starter information on cards for their Venn diagram.

Implementation

- In small groups or pairs, students are given a set of Hands-On Venn Diagram cards.
- Students can be provided with a blank Venn diagram board, draw their own on paper, or make a temporary yarn circle on their desk.
- Students are given the titles for the two circles and must first discuss and then place the cards into each area of their Venn diagram.

Specific Uses or Ideas

- *Preassessment*: As students prepare to study a significant event in their state's history during social studies class, they are given a set of Hands-On

Venn Diagram cards. Each group or pair of students is asked to place the cards containing information about that event into the Hands-On Venn Diagram circles entitled "At the Start of the Event" and "Near the End of the Event." The intersection of the two circles represents various things that occurred throughout the event itself (and not in just one specific instance). Once students complete the Hands-On Venn Diagram, they can record their information, make their own Venn diagram to organize information learned during the unit, or share their placements of the cards with the rest of the class in a discussion format.

- *Discussion*: During a unit on nutrition in science class, Hands-On Venn Diagram cards can be used in order to reinforce the different food groups on the food pyramid and the food found within these groups. Students are given a set of Hands-On Venn Diagram cards and are asked to label their Venn diagram circles with "Bread and Cereal Group" and "Milk Group." Then each group discusses the foods on their cards and places their cards in the appropriate circle. The cards contain recipes, descriptions, or pictures of simple foods, as well as complex foods, that cross into the two groups. Each group discusses the items on its cards and places them appropriately. Once groups have placed their cards, each food item is discussed again to increase the students' understanding of the food pyramid.

- *Independent Practice*: During a math lesson on multiples, pairs of students are given a set of Hands-On Venn Diagram cards. Their Venn diagram circles are labeled with "6" and "8." The pairs are then given sets of cards, which contains multiples of each number as well as a few numbers that do not fit into any of the circles. Students discuss each number, its placement, and the reasoning behind the placement. Students will discover and share patterns on their own. The lesson can also go on to explain that the least common multiple is the lowest number in the intersection of the two circles in the Hands-On Venn Diagram.

- *Review*: Most units of study in language arts class ask students to compare and contrast events, characters, or concepts found in a piece of literature. Therefore, creating a Hands-On Venn Diagram is a very effective way of bringing the big picture back into the concept review. In order to review for a test over a novel they have studied, students complete a Hands-On Venn Diagram that has them compare and contrast the settings and events before and after the climax of the story.

- *Anchor Activity*: After finishing a unit or lesson, students often enjoy the opportunity to create their own Hands-On Venn Diagram cards for their classmates. On the computer, set up a blank document with a table template, and have students enter their own lists of items they have brainstormed, print them out, and create a Hands-On Venn Diagram for others to complete as they finish their lesson.

Materials

- Cardstock or colored paper

Directions for Creating a Hands-On Venn Diagram

- Determine the objectives that will need to be compared and contrasted through the Hands-On Venn Diagram activity. These objectives could be expressed through vocabulary words, large conceptual ideas, or special content-based phrases. Brainstorm a master list of the information that will be included on the Hands-On Venn Diagram cards.
- Once the list has been brainstormed, enter the items into a table, using the word processing program of your choice.
- Once the master list has been created, print or copy the list onto different sets of colored paper, making each copy a different color. This will allow stray cards to be returned quickly to their original set.
- Cut apart each set of Hands-On Venn Diagram cards and place each set into its own plastic bag. Depending on how the cards are being used, different numbers of sets will be needed. For example, using them at a center may require only two sets total, whereas using them with the whole group broken into pairs may require up to 15.

Modifications

- Students can be given the challenge to determine what should be represented in each circle given the words or phrases on the cards.

Sample Explanation

- The following page has sample Hands-On Venn Diagram cards for nouns and verbs, as well as a sample Hands-On Venn Diagram with categories included. These words were chosen specifically to allow for varying levels of understanding as students discuss the words that fit in the intersection of the two circles.

Nouns and Verbs Hands-On Venn Diagram Cards

Bottle	Explain	Narrate
Breakfast	Find	Paper
Brush	Grade	Plane
Cactus	Greet	Plant
Cat	Heat	Rain
Circle	Help	Ride
Defend	Lamp	Run
Doctor	Locate	Test
Earn	Mail	Wind
Elect	Month	Write

Ready-to-Use Differentiation Strategies, Grades 3–5 © Taylor & Francis.

Nouns and Verbs Hands-On Venn Diagram

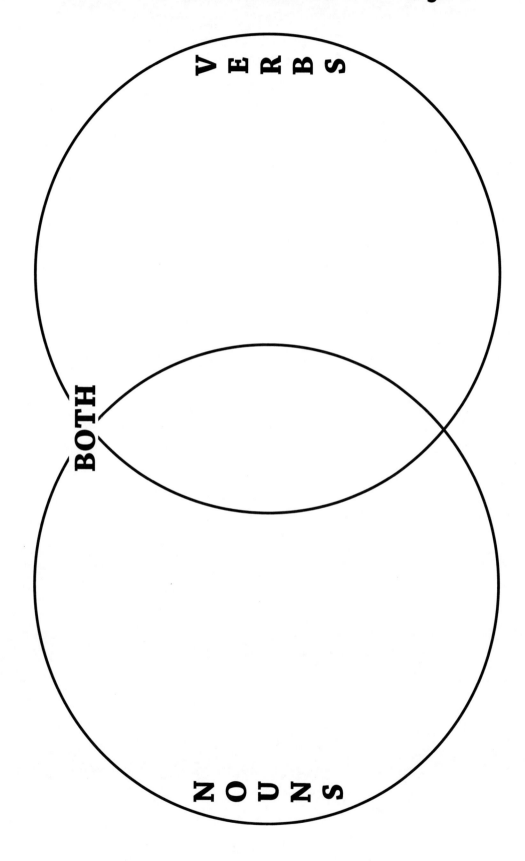

MYTH VERSUS REALITY

Learning Styles Accommodated

- Auditory
- Tactile/Kinesthetic
- Verbal

Best Practices

- Preassessment
- Discussion
- Independent Practice
- Review
- Extension

Description

- In Myth Versus Reality, students are asked to determine if a statement is a myth or reality and share why they selected that response.

Implementation

- Students are given a list of three to five statements.
- They read the statements individually and decide if the statements are myths or realities.
- Once they have recorded their ideas, they are allowed to discuss one of the statements with their group. (Although students are told they are to discuss just one of the statements, they often "sneak" a few more statements into the discussion.)
- Responses can be debated within the group, discussed with the whole group, researched, or simply defended and turned in for grading.

Specific Uses or Ideas

- *Preassessment*: Myth Versus Reality has obvious uses as a preassessment tool. Statements and ideas from the unit of study can be selected for the activity. Students are asked to determine if the statement is a myth or reality and to defend their answer. These statements and defenses can be used to build background knowledge or as a tool to compact the curriculum for students who already know the material.

- *Discussion*: Before a unit is started, Myth Versus Reality can be used to pique student interest, build background knowledge, and encourage discussion. For example, before studying the Revolutionary War in social studies class, a Myth Versus Reality can be designed with statements about the culture of that period, from communication methods and battlefield medicine, to the efficiency of the weapons. Students determine whether the statements are myth or reality and then discuss and defend their ideas. As answers are revealed, the discussion helps to enrich students' background knowledge before going further into the unit.

- *Independent Practice*: Myth Versus Reality can be used as independent practice in a number of ways, but it can be quite beneficial for the "show your work" battle that often takes place in the math classroom. A Myth Versus Reality can be developed for a math lesson in which the problem is stated with a specific answer. For example, a Myth Versus Reality statement might be:

  > Anna had 5 feet of ribbon that was cut into 3 sections without any left over. Each section was 1.25 feet.

  In order for students to prove that this statement is a myth, they will have to show the steps of the problem. If it were a reality, they would still have to show how they obtained that response. Although giving the answer may seem to defeat the purpose of the problem, students have to work through all of the steps to determine its validity.

- *Review*: Vague or debatable statements about content found in the current unit work best with Myth Versus Reality. By choosing these types of statements for the review, there is more opportunity for discussion and debate as statements are interpreted and answers are shared. The more students discuss and debate the material, the more they will remember and understand.

- *Extension*: At the beginning of the unit, students are given a Myth Versus Reality with extension statements over the current material. They are asked to determine if the statements are myths or realities; however, they must find documented evidence to support their responses. Near the end of the unit, the students bring their statements, responses, and all of the research they have located to back up and debate their points of view. This is an excellent opportunity to discuss reliable sources, as well as primary and secondary sources if appropriate.

Materials

- Myth Versus Reality statements

Modifications

- Statements can reflect other dichotomies, such as true or false, living or nonliving, and support or dispute.

Sample Explanation

- The following pages have examples of generic Myth Versus Realities that can be used for prereading, postreading, and science experiments (this sheet would be partially filled out before the students begin the lab, with the remaining portion to be filled out during and after the lab). These templates can be used as they are or modified to meet the students' needs.

Prereading Myth Versus Reality

Write the title and author of your reading.

_____

_____

Consider the title of your reading and mark each statement with Myth (M) or Reality (R). Write a sentence to explain why you think the statement is a myth or reality.

_____ 1. This story could happen in real life.

_____

_____

_____ 2. This story is interesting.

_____

_____

_____ 3. The main character is strong.

_____

_____

_____ 4. Something exciting will happen in this story.

_____

_____

_____ 5. The author wrote this story to entertain.

_____

_____

After reading the book, are there any statements above you would now change? Which ones and why?

_____

_____

_____

_____

_____

_____

Postreading Myth Versus Reality

Write the title and author of your reading.

_____

_____

Considering what you have read, mark each statement with Myth (M) or Reality (R). Write a sentence to explain why you think the statement is a myth or reality.

_____ 1. The setting of the story is important to the plot.

_____

_____

_____ 2. This story is interesting.

_____

_____

_____ 3. The main character did the right thing.

_____

_____

_____ 4. The title of the story is well chosen.

_____

_____

_____ 5. The author enjoyed writing this story.

_____

_____

Science Experiment Myth Versus Reality

Write the title of the science lab.

_____

_____

Consider the title of the science lab and mark each statement with Myth (M) or Reality (R). Write a brief sentence to explain why you feel the statement is a myth or reality.

_____ 1. There are no specific safety rules for this activity.

_____

_____

_____ 2. We are only using equipment I have used before.

_____

_____

_____ 3. All of the procedures make sense.

_____

_____

_____ 4. This activity is related to what we are talking about in class.

_____

_____

_____ 5. My group worked well together on this activity.

_____

_____

NAILING THE MAIL

Learning Styles Accommodated

- Auditory
- Tactile/Kinesthetic
- Verbal
- Visual

Best Practices

- Preassessment
- 10–2
- Discussion
- Independent Practice
- Review

Description

- In Nailing the Mail, groups of students receive envelopes with questions or prompts written on them and take turns anonymously answering them and passing the envelope to the next group to answer as well. For the last envelope they receive, groups rank all of the responses to the question or prompt found on the envelope.

Implementation

- Students are broken into groups of three or four students. Each group is given a number and a pile of index cards.
- The group should put its group number in the upper right-hand corner of each index card.
- Each group is given an envelope with a content-related question or prompt written on the outside of the envelope.
- The group reads and discusses the question or prompt. Once the group has determined its answer, a student will write it on one of the group's index cards and place it back in the envelope.
- After time has been called, the envelopes rotate to the next group in the sequence, so that each group receives a new question. Again, each group

considers its response to the new "mail" question or prompt, records it on one of its numbered index cards, and places it in the envelope.

- This process continues until the groups have used all of their cards and have received their last envelope. At this point, the group will open the envelope and remove all of the cards inside.
- After reading all of the cards inside the envelope, the group ranks the cards from the most effective to least effective answer and, using a marker, awards points to each card based on its rank. The highest ranked answer would receive the most points (e.g., if there are eight groups, the highest ranked response would receive eight points, the next highest seven, and so on, through the last card, which would receives one point).
- After ranking the responses, each group is given the opportunity to read the question or prompt from the envelope it ranked, share the top-ranked answer, and defend why the group selected that answer as the most effective.
- The envelopes can then be picked up and the cards returned to groups by their group number. The groups can add up their points for each ranking for their total Nail the Mail points.

Specific Uses or Ideas

- *Preassessment*: When using Nail the Mail for a preassessment strategy, the questions or prompts written on the outside of the envelopes should focus on building background knowledge or assessing what students remember from previous years. Examples might be:
  o Name as many vocabulary words as you can about sound.
  o Draw a food chain.
  o Describe the water cycle.
  o What are fractions?
  o Why should we study [objective from upcoming unit]?

- *10–2*: Nail the Mail can be used as a 10–2 strategy by handing out the envelopes to the groups at the beginning of the lesson. During the 2-minute processing time, students respond to the envelope's question or prompt on their index card, place it in the envelope, and switch. They will read and respond to the next question or prompt during the next 2-minute break for processing. When using Nail the Mail this way, it is imperative that the questions posted on the envelope can be answered without having exposure to the entire lesson.
- *Discussion*: When using Nail the Mail as a discussion tool, questions or prompts are chosen to encourage discussion about the topic at hand. The groups may need a little more time to discuss the question or prompt on

the envelope before composing their responses and then additional time to rank the cards in the envelopes. Examples of discussion items may include:

o   What historical figure had the most impact on our country? Defend your answer.

o   Why should we study _____?

o   Explaining _____ is the easiest part of this unit because . . .

o   If your group had to teach your classmates about _____, what is the most important thing to remember?

- *Independent Practice*: Nail the Mail is effective in any independent practice activity, but it is especially effective in proofreading. Each group is given a card with a different proofreading strategy, such as grammar check (with specific requirements), add two adjectives, or make two positive suggestions to improve the writing. Instead of rotating envelopes containing cards and a question, the envelopes will contain written works by members of each group. Each member of a group will put his group's number on his written work and place it in the group's envelope. Each group passes its envelope to the next group. That group will open the envelope, distribute the written works inside, and proofread them using the proofreading strategy written on its card. This can be done individually or with group support. After time has passed, the written works are placed back into the envelopes and rotated to another group, which will proofread the works using the unique strategy on its card. This continues until the written works have worked their way through every group and are returned to their home group. This group can exchange papers themselves, complete the proofreading task using the strategy on its own card, and return each paper full of comments to its owner.

- *Review*: Nail the Mail is an obvious tool for review. Any questions or prompts that could be put on review sheets could be placed on the outside of the envelopes. If there are more questions than groups, the teacher can collect envelopes after they have gone through all groups and each group can rank more than one envelope. It is up to the teacher if the students can leave their own answer in the envelope during the ranking or not.

Materials

- Envelopes (one for each group)
- Index cards (each group needs one fewer card than there are groups)

Directions for Creating Nail the Mail

- Write an open-ended content-related question or prompt that can be solved in different ways on the outside of the envelope. It is important when using this with problems that there be more than one correct solution to the problem.
- Index cards can be counted and stacked for groups to save time during the activity.

Modifications

- The first group to have the envelope can create a problem or write an open-ended question for the other groups to answer.

PRIORITIZATION FLAP BOOK

Learning Styles Accommodated

- Auditory
- Tactile/Kinesthetic
- Verbal
- Visual

Best Practices

- Independent Practice
- Review
- Extension

Description

- The Prioritization Flap Book asks students to prioritize ideas, concepts, or problems being studied and to provide information supporting their rankings.

Implementation

- Students are given a priority brainstorming outline or work together with the large group to brainstorm ideas, concepts, or problems from the content being covered.
- Once ideas, concepts, or problems have been brainstormed, each student is asked to rank or order the information. All students can use the same ranking criteria, or students can rank the information in many different ways, including:
  - o   easiest to hardest,
  - o   slowest to fastest,
  - o   least dangerous to most dangerous,
  - o   least important to most important,
  - o   least helpful to most helpful,

> o   least plentiful to most plentiful, and
> o   least popular to most popular.

- Depending on the students' levels, they can spend more time brainstorming to solidify their understanding of the reasons behind their ranking.
- Students are provided paper to assemble their Prioritization Flap Book based on the number of items that will be placed on the flaps.
- Students record the prioritized items on the flaps of the book, placing the most important item on the bottom flap; this flap has the greatest amount of space for writing.

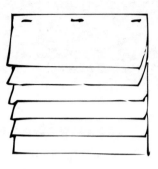

Prioritization Flap Book example

Specific Uses or Ideas

- *Independent Practice*: Prioritization Flap Books work well with concepts or examples that have obvious sequences or tiers, such as levels of government or levels of organization. They can, however, provide a deeper level of understanding when used with content not often prioritized. For example, after discussing the types of simple machines in science class, students are asked to prioritize the different types by considering how today's world would be altered if the machines did not exist. For language arts, students can be given a statement to prove using textual evidence after reading a chapter in a novel. They complete a Prioritization Flap Book in which they select quotes from the story and rank them from providing the least support to providing the most support for the given statement.
- *Review*: To review content that might be found on an assessment, students brainstorm questions about the current unit of study. They need to rank the questions from most basic (e.g., a multiple-choice question) to most complex (e.g., an essay question). They record their questions on the flaps of their Prioritization Flap Book and place the answers with an explanation on the inside. Because the answers are on the inside, students are also self-checking when they exchange their Prioritization Flap Books to quiz each other
- *Extension*: Once students have completed a unit of study, they can begin investigating cross-curricular connections. Students can use their Prioritization Flap Books to rank how the present unit of study relates to their other classes. For example, after studying fractions in math class, students list all of their other classes and brainstorm how fractions might be used in each content area. They rank these ideas from least useful to

most useful and provide examples of how fractions are used in each class on the inside flap of the Prioritization Flap Book.

Materials

- Letter-sized paper

Directions for Creating a Prioritization Flap Book

- Determine the number of items (therefore the number of pages) students will need to prioritize on their flap book. The amount of paper needed is as follows:
  - o Three or four items will use two pieces of paper.
  - o Five or six items will use three pieces of paper.
  - o Seven or eight items will use four pieces of paper.
  - o Nine items will use five pieces of paper.

Step 1

- **Step 1:** Students should place the first piece of paper on the table in front of them with the short side facing them.

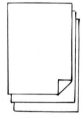

Step 2

- **Step 2:** The next piece is placed on top of the first, leaving about 3/4 of an inch of the first paper showing at the bottom. The next paper is place on top of the other two, again leaving 3/4 of an inch of the second paper showing. This continues until all of the paper is placed.

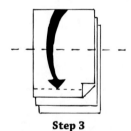

Step 3

- **Step 3:** Then, take the top of the papers and fold them down to meet the bottom, leaving 3/4 of an inch between the bottom of the last placed page and the top of the folded paper. This creates flaps for student ideas and writing.

- **Step 4:** Staple across the top of the book to keep pages in place.

Step 4

Modifications

- Prioritization Flap Books with letter-sized paper allow sufficient space for up to five items; for nine items, legal-sized paper provides enough space. If students need to prioritize more than nine items, larger paper will be needed to accommodate the material and allow enough room to write about each item.

Sample Explanation

- The following page has a sample prioritization brainstorming activity that can be used as is or modified to meet the students' needs.

Prioritization Brainstorm

Name the ideas you will be ranking.

_____   _____

_____   _____

_____   _____

_____   _____

How will your ideas be ranked?

_____

_____

The smallest flap will be your lowest ranked item, and the largest flap will be the highest ranked item. Record your rankings and your reasons for their placement below.

Smallest Flap: _____ Example: _____

Why did you place this here? _____

_____

_____

Second Flap: _____ Example: _____

Why did you place this here? _____

_____

_____

Third Flap: _____ Example: _____

Why did you place this here? _____

_____

_____

Fourth Flap: _____ Example: _____

Why did you place this here? _____

_____

_____

Largest Flap: _____ Example: _____

Why did you place this here? _____

_____

_____

RED LIGHT, GREEN LIGHT

Learning Styles Accommodated

- Tactile/Kinesthetic
- Verbal
- Visual

Best Practices

- Preassessment
- Discussion
- Checking for Understanding
- Guided Practice
- Review

Description

- In Red Light, Green Light, students display a red or green paddle to show their response to a question, situation, or discussion point.

Implementation

- Groups of students are given a set of Red Light, Green Light paddles.
- Groups are asked to briefly discuss a question, situation, or discussion point. The group must come to a consensus and display its response paddle. The colors can relate to various responses, including:
  o We agree (green); we disagree (red).
  o We believe it is true (green); we believe it is false (red).
  o We understand (green); it is still confusing (red).
  o We have agreement in our group (green); we cannot reach a consensus (red).
  o The answer is an even or positive number (green); the answer an odd or negative number (red).
  o Any two categories that are being studied.

- Once groups have raised their paddles, any responses can be discussed or shared.

Specific Uses or Ideas

- *Preassessment*: When beginning a unit on fractions in math class, a set of statements about fractions and their properties is prepared in advance to refresh students on the content they learned the previous year. Students are placed in pairs and are given a set of the Red Light, Green Light paddles. As each prepared statement is presented, each pair shares its green paddle to express understanding or agreement or its red paddle to express confusion or disagreement.

- *Discussion*: During a novel study in language arts class, students briefly pause during the reading to respond to discussion questions about the plot and make predictions about the characters and their actions.

- *Checking for Understanding*: Students are provided with the Red Light, Green Light paddles at the beginning of a lesson and are periodically asked to show their colored paddles to reflect the difficulty of the information as it is presented. Students are sometimes reticent to share when they do not understand something, so paddles can be held in front of their bodies or shown on the count of three.

- *Guided Practice*: After being introduced to the proper use of commas in a series in language arts class, students are shown examples of commas in a series used both correctly and incorrectly. As each sentence is shown, groups are asked to discuss whether the sentence is correct (green) or incorrect (red) and show the appropriate-colored paddle. If the sentence is incorrect, the group should prepare a corrected version of the sentence for sharing.

- *Review*: Red Light, Green Light can be used individually or with small groups while reviewing concepts, depending on the types of questions being asked. Teachers may want to have students sit on the floor facing forward and hold their paddles in their lap so they are only visible to the teacher. If the paddles are to be shown, it is helpful to provide students with the review questions ahead of time so they can prepare to participate in the activity.

Materials

- Red and green paper or cardstock
- Craft sticks
- White school glue

Directions for Creating Right Light, Green Light

- Although there are various options for creating the response paddles, here is one suggestion:
  o   Obtain enough pieces of red and green cardstock for everyone to have one of each color.
  o   Fold each piece of cardstock in half, hamburger style.
  o   Place the craft stick between the folded pages and glue them securely closed. Allow approximately half of the craft stick to extend past the bottom of the folded cards for a handle.

Modifications

- A third (yellow) paddle could be added to the set to allow for three options, including:
  o   Strongly agree (green), strongly disagree (red), and no opinion (yellow).
  o   True (green), false (red), and depends (yellow).

- Red Light, Green Light is a great accompaniment to the Myth Versus Reality strategy found on page 99.

TOY SHARE

Learning Styles Accommodated

- Auditory
- Tactile/Kinesthetic
- Visual

Best Practices

- Preassessment
- 10–2
- Discussion
- Review
- Anchor Activity
- Extension

Description

- Toy Share is a ready-to-use strategy in which students are given various toys or other interesting objects and asked to make a creative association between the toy and a concept from the content being studied.

Implementation

- Have each student, pair, or group jot down four or five facts about the topic being studied.
- Each student, pair, or group selects or receives a random toy or interesting object.
- Students are challenged to make an association between the toy and the facts they recorded earlier. For example, "A spinning top is like the Revolutionary War because a top is/has _____ and the war is/has _____." Not all students need a structural hint sentence.
- Once students have developed their association sentence, they can share their sentence with the larger group.
- After each group has shared, hold up the various toys and have students recall how each was associated with the topic at hand to help cement the associations.

Specific Uses or Ideas

- *Preassessment*: On the first day of a science unit on adaptations, groups of students receive a toy and are asked to show how it is related to the idea of adaptations based on their prior knowledge.
- *10–2*: At the beginning of a lesson, students are divided into groups of two or three. Each group receives a unique object that it will use throughout the lesson. As information is presented and instruction pauses for the 2-minute processing time, each group is asked to brainstorm how its object is related to a concept that was just presented.
- *Discussion*: The teacher selects one unique or creative toy and shows it to the class. After the teacher has presented the lesson, each group is asked to create an association between the current content and the unique toy and share it with the whole class. Once all of the groups have shared, the class can then evaluate the ideas and rank the proposed associations.
- *Review*: After being divided into pairs, students are given one of the concepts covered during the unit. They should record three to four different ideas about the concept. They can then select a toy or interesting object and create an association between that object and the given concept. Once the associations are created, each pair can share its associations. On the day of the assessment, toys are placed around the classroom for a visual reminder of the associations.
- *Anchor Activity*: Place a bucket containing 10–15 toys or interesting items in a central location. As students finish their work, they can select an item from the bucket and create an association for that item as it relates to what was discussed that day and then illustrate it. These can be collected, posted, shared, or made into a class book.
- *Extension*: Students find 10–15 household items (or toys in catalogs or at home) that they can associate creatively with the content currently being studied. These items can be presented in an exhibit with their association statements. They can also be made into a children's book. For example, a page from a toy share extension book on fractions might read, "A sports action figure is like a fraction because it is part of a whole—its team."

Materials

- Lots of free, interesting, unique objects or toys

Directions for Creating Toy Share

- Begin accumulating various small toys; this is the chance to find toys that make noise, light up, move, or are otherwise considered "annoying."

Inexpensive toys can be found in fast food children's meals, at garage sales, or in thrift stores.

- A great toy bucket would have more than 25 different toys or interesting objects, such as handheld eggbeaters, a small bubble level, and other small objects students may not have experienced before.

Modifications

- Groups can be any size, although the larger the groups are, the more likely students may be to agree with the rest of group rather than asserting their own creative ideas.
- The same toy can be given to more than one group. Groups can then share and compare their ideas with each other.

WEB CARDS

Learning Styles Accommodated

- Tactile/Kinesthetic
- Verbal
- Visual

Best Practices

- Preassessment
- Independent Practice
- Review
- Anchor Activity

Description

- Web Cards are a kinesthetic, interactive version of mind mapping or webbing.

Implementation

- Students should be paired up or separated into groups of three. Each group is given a set of Web Cards.
- Each group is asked to create a web based on the following guidelines:
  o Students must use all of the cards, with the exception of the free space, which is optional.
  o Everyone in the group must be able to defend or explain the group's placement of cards.
  o Everyone in the group must agree on the placement of the cards.
  o No more than four! (In other words, no more than four words can be coming off of any other card—one going in, and up to three coming out. See example below.)

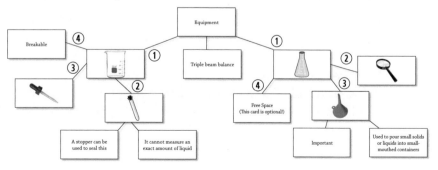

- After the guidelines are explained, it helps to indicate that there are more than 47 (or any other number you want to make up!) different correct combinations. This will free students from worrying that their webs are different from their classmates' because there are so many right answers.
- Once a group is finished, it can compare its web with another group's, do a gallery walk, or discuss how cards were placed with the whole group. After these opportunities, students can record their web permanently on a poster or in their notebooks.

Specific Uses or Ideas

- *Preassessment*: Before any instruction has taken place, students are given a bag of Web Cards with key words from the unit. After the guidelines are explained, students assemble their web to the best of their ability based on their prior knowledge. If these webs are written on Post-It notes, they can be arranged and rearranged as the unit progresses.
- *Independent Practice*: After discussing the relationship between decimals and fractions, students are given a set of 15 Web Cards containing sample decimals, sample equivalent fractions, definitions, and the word *sports car*. Students work in pairs to create a web. As the teacher circulates, he or she will ask completed pairs to explain their use of the word sports car before having students recording their web in their notebooks.
- *Review*: After spending time working with Web Cards, students can create a set of cards to be used to review all of the content in the unit. These cards can be exchanged with classmates, and once they have completed each other's cards, students can discuss the different interpretations of the information.
- *Anchor Activity*: After finishing their work, students can challenge each other by creating their own Web Cards for the current unit.

Materials

- Cardstock or colored paper

Directions for Creating Web Cards

- Choose 15–30 concepts from the current unit of study. These concepts could be vocabulary words, pictures, topics, definitions, main ideas, examples, and other significant tidbits of information. It is best to randomly choose words and concepts without knowing or predicting how the web should look. This makes it easier to accept and appreciate modifications that the students create. Another level of depth can be added by including a free space card and two creative association words that are not related to the present unit, such as marshmallow, lamp, or sports car. By using these words, students will have to think of possible creative associations between the content and these words.

- Write or type these concepts on cardstock and print or copy the card sets on different colors of cardstock, so any loose cards that are found can be returned to their stack.
- Cut out the cards and place them in clear plastic bags.

Modifications

- The number of cards can be changed based on the students' ability levels. The more cards there are, the more complex the activity becomes because of the "no more than four" rule.
- Separate bags of colored arrows can be created and kept for students who prefer to see visible connections between cards. If Web Cards are going to be used more than once during the school year, it is helpful to create a class set of these arrow-filled bags and keep them handy.
- Free choice and creative association (words not directly related to the topic) cards can be used at the discretion of the teacher.
- Students can work independently on the Web Cards. They miss the active discussion during creation, but they can share theirs with someone else at their table or nearby. Students can look for similarities and differences between their webs and can explain why they made the connections that they made.

Sample Explanation

- On the pages that follow is a set of scientific equipment Web Cards. There are judgment words (e.g., important), as well as pictures, definitions, facts, and even the word marshmallow. Although this web may seem incomplete and other words or concepts could be included, by excluding certain obvious concepts, it makes the web and its interconnections more challenging. There is not an answer key included with this web, as there are many different combinations (perhaps more than 24, but this number is just stated to make students feel better), all based on how the students defend their placement of the location of the cards.

Science Equipment Web Cards

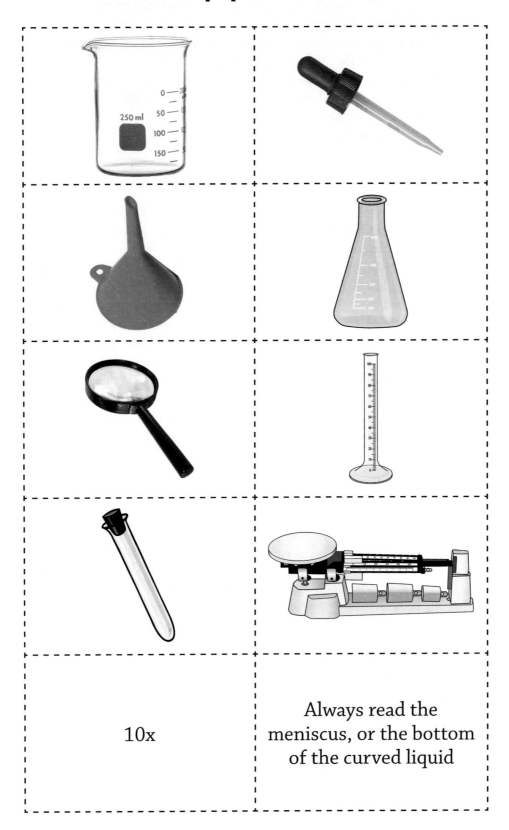

10x

Always read the meniscus, or the bottom of the curved liquid

Science Equipment Web Cards

A stopper can be used to seal this	It cannot measure an exact amount of liquid
Breakable	Important
Equipment	Measure
Eyedropper	Triple beam balance
Free space (This card is optional!)	Marshmallow

Science Equipment Web Cards

Funnel	Liquid
Made of either plastic or glass	Used to pour small solids or liquids into small-mouthed containers
Solid	Beaker
Used for transporting small amounts of liquid	Glassware
Used to determine the mass of an object	Allows you to look closely at objects

RESOURCES

Brighton, C. M. (2005, Fall). Preassessment: A differentiation power tool. *Teaching for High Potential*, 2–4.

Chapman, C., & Gregory, G. H. (2002). *Differentiated instructional strategies: One size doesn't fit all*. Thousand Oaks, CA: Corwin Press.

Coil, C. (2007). *Successful teaching in the differentiated classroom*. Marion, IL: Pieces of Learning.

Coleman, M. R., & Gallagher, J. J. (1995). Appropriate differentiated services: Guides for best practices in the education of gifted children. *Gifted Child Today, 18*(5), 32–33.

Hunter, M. (1994). *Enhancing teaching*. New York, NY: Macmillan.

Kingore, B. (2004). *Differentiation: Simplified, realistic, and effective*. Austin, TX: Professional Associates.

Langer, G. M. (2004). *Teaching as decision making: Successful practices for the secondary teacher* (2nd ed.). Upper Saddle River, NJ: Pearson/Merrill Prentice Hall.

Maker, C. J. (1982). *Curriculum development for the gifted*. Rockville, MD: Aspen.

Rutherford, P. (2002). *Instruction for all students*. Alexandria, VA: Just ASK Publications.

Slocumb, P. D., & Monaco, T. (1986, November/December). Differentiating the curriculum. *Gifted Child Today*, 30–34.

Tomlinson, C. A. (1995). *How to differentiate instruction in mixed-ability classrooms*. Alexandria, VA: Association for Supervision and Curriculum Development.

Tomlinson, C. A. (1999). *The differentiated classroom: Responding to the needs of all learners*. Alexandria, VA: Association for Supervision and Curriculum Development.

Tomlinson, C. A., & Imbeau, M. B. (2010). *Leading and managing a differentiated classroom*. Alexandria, VA: ASCD.

Westberg, K. L., & Archambault, F. X., Jr. (1997). A multi-site case study of successful classroom practices for high ability students. *Gifted Child Quarterly, 41*, 42–51.

Winebrenner, S. (1992). *Teaching gifted kids in the regular classroom: Strategies and techniques every teacher can use to meet the academic needs of the gifted and talented*. Minneapolis, MN: Free Spirit.

ABOUT THE AUTHOR

After teaching science for more than 15 years, both overseas and in the U.S., **Laurie E. Westphal** now works as an independent gifted education and science consultant nationwide. She enjoys developing and presenting staff development on differentiation for various districts and conferences, working with teachers to assist them in planning and developing lessons to meet the needs of their advanced students. Laurie currently resides in Houston, TX, and has made it her goal to convert as many teachers as she can to the differentiated lifestyle in the classroom and share her vision for real-world, product-based lessons that help all students become critical thinkers and effective problem solvers. She is the author of the Differentiating Instruction With Menus series, as well as *Hands-On Physical Science* and *Science Dictionary for Kids*.